# PERSPECTIVES ON EARLY CHILDHOOD PSYCHOLOGY AND EDUCATION

## SPECIAL FOCUS

## Prevention of Behavioral and Emotional Disorders in Early Childhood

Volume 3, Issue 1
Spring 2018

ISBN: 978-1-935625-28-5
ISSN: 2471-1527

Member
Council of Editors of Learned Journals

CELJ

Special thanks to graduate assistant Claire Seeger and

editorial assistant Gina Cooper for their work on this issue of *PECPE*

# PERSPECTIVES on EARLY CHILDHOOD PSYCHOLOGY and EDUCATION

# TABLE OF CONTENTS

## SPECIAL FOCUS: PREVENTION OF BEHAVIORAL AND EMOTIONAL DISORDERS IN EARLY CHILDHOOD

# Introduction and Editor's Note

In this special focus issue of *Perspectives on Early Childhood Psychology and Education* (*PECPE*) guest editors Melissa Stormont and Laine Young-Walker include several manuscripts on prevention of behavioral and emotional disorders in early childhood. More specifically, topics such as the creation of interdisciplinary prevention efforts on a wide scale within a local community, the importance and strategies to increase early screening using evidence based tools, and coordinated and systematic ways to create sustainable change in different early childhood settings are addressed. I am thankful to them for preparing an excellent issue for researchers, practitioners, and students alike.

We are seeking a special focus for the fall 2018 issue of *PECPE*. If you are interested in submitting a topic and being the guest editor, please send a brief (approximately 250 words) proposal to me (see contact information below) for consideration. Special focus and general manuscripts for the fall 2018 issue are due **August 15, 2018**. Manuscripts should be original work not currently submitted for publication to other journals. Authors must follow the guidelines of the *Publication Manual of the American Psychological Association* (Sixth Edition). Manuscripts may not exceed 35 double-spaced pages in length, including the cover page, abstract, references, tables, and figures. Avoid including any identifying author information in the text. Selection of manuscripts is based on blind peer review. Include a cover page with the following information: the title of article, author(s) full name(s), title(s), institution or professional affiliations, and mailing and email address of primary author. The cover page will not be sent to reviewers.

Readers who are interested in becoming a member of the editorial board of *PECPE* should contact me via email at PECPE@gonzaga.edu or alfonso@gonzaga.edu. In closing, we hope you find *PECPE* to be a useful journal in your research and practice. Please feel free to contact us with ideas, comments, and suggestions.

We are very open to innovative ideas and look forward to hearing from you.

Enjoy *PECPE*!
Vincent C. Alfonso, Ph.D.
Editor

# Prevention of Behavioral and Emotional Disorders in Early Childhood

# Introduction to the Special Focus: Prevention of Behavior Disorders

*Melissa Stormont and Laine Young-Walker*

Emotional and behavioral problems have been associated with a number of negative outcomes for children, youth, families, and societies (Centers for Disease Control and Prevention [CDC], 2013; Darney, Reinke, Herman, Stormont, & Ialongo, 2013). Children who enter kindergarten with early emotional and behavioral problems are often met with school expectations that exacerbate their problems (Stormont, Reinke, Herman, & Lembke, 2012; Zins, Bloodworth, Weissberg, & Walberg, 2007). If challenging behavior problems continue throughout the early childhood years, the likelihood of school suspension, failure, drop out, incarceration, and other negative outcomes increases (Darney et al., 2013; Dowdy, Ritchey, & Kamphaus, 2010).

Therefore, it is imperative that early childhood professionals are well versed in identifying and remediating early behavior problems. It is also critical that interdisciplinary efforts are utilized to adequately study and intervene with this population, who may face multifaceted and idiosyncratic problems that require support across different programs. This special focus addresses ways to screen for and employ early intervention to prevent and ameliorate behavior problems. Many of the articles focus on the importance of interdisciplinary efforts to address the multifaceted issues often faced by young children and their families and the systemic needs for programs that serve children.

Articles in this special focus address screening, prevention, and intervention across multiple areas. In the first article, Oakes and colleagues present a model for using universal behavior screening to determine and support children who need more support. Universal social-behavioral screening in early childhood is an important area for prevention models, as the use of comprehensive screening supports professional use of more empirical means for determining support and follow-up assessment needs. The need to apply data-based decisions regarding which children require different levels of support is also addressed in this article and applied examples are provided.

Combining screening and interventions across multiple systems, in the next article Stormont and colleagues present a large-scale community effort to build systemic change in a local community. Utilizing best practices to adopt, employ, and monitor progress, community representatives and the researchers formed a wellness council that provided guidance, buy in, and support across each of the jointly determined prevention and intervention goals. Goals selected included increased screening for social-emotional health in young children, parenting interventions, and support for child-care providers to increase their use of social-emotional screening and positive behavior support strategies.

Another important consideration for prevention of behavior problems and disorders is use of culturally appropriate practices across all agencies and professionals who work with young children and their families. Historically, children of color are overrepresented in referrals for disciplinary action and evaluations for disabilities. Change is required to support more equitable treatment in agencies and schools that serve young children of color. Green and colleagues outline how practices can be supported and implemented within the classroom and in outreach efforts to engage families.

Walker and a team of researchers discuss recent research on First Step, including the iterative process and preliminary research on First Step Next. First Step Next is a collaborative Tier II program which focuses on school readiness skills. The article provides a comprehensive description of the process by which First Step was revised as well as needs for future research. This work is important to support prevention efforts for behavior disorders—including adapting a highly effective intervention for the changing needs of the school setting—and to align the intervention with current prevention-based models such as school-wide positive behavior supports and interventions.

In their article, Schultz and colleagues discuss the importance of supporting evidence-based parenting practices for children with autism spectrum disorder (ASD). It is critical that young children with disabilities are not overlooked in prevention-based efforts given their characteristics and, in fact, children with autism have been very responsive to evidence-based interventions targeting social behavior needs. It is also imperative that parents of children with ASD are provided with such interventions and supports, given that they report high levels of parenting stress.

The final special issue article also focuses on parenting interventions. Dyches and colleagues conducted a meta-analysis of the impact of parenting interventions on children with developmental disabilities. The three outcome variables of interest were social skills, life skills/adaptive behavior, and communication skills. Thirty studies were included in the analysis. Significant findings were documented for parenting interventions and implications are discussed related to how findings can direct interventions.

## References

Centers for Disease Control and Prevention (2013). Mental health surveillance among children—United States, 2005–2011. *Morbidity and Mortality Weekly Report, 62*, 1–35. Retrieved from www.cdc.gov

Darney, D., Reinke, W. M., Herman, K. C., Stormont, M., & Ialongo, N. (2013). Children with co-occurring academic and behavior problems in 1st grade: Distal outcomes in 12th grade. *Journal of School Psychology, 51*(1), 117–128.

Dowdy, E., Ritchey, K., & Kamphaus, R. W. (2010). School-based screening: A population-based approach to inform and monitor children's mental health needs. *School Mental Health, 2*(4), 166–176.

Stormont, M., Reinke, W., Herman, K., & Lembke, E. (2012). *Tier two interventions: Academic and behavior supports for children at risk for failure.* New York, NY: Guilford.

Zins, J. E., Bloodworth, M. R., Weissberg, R. P., & Walberg, H. J. (2007). The scientific base linking social and emotional learning to school success. *Journal of Educational and Psychological Consultation, 17*(2–3), 191–210.

# Systematic Screening for Behavior in Early Childhood Settings: Early Identification and Intervention within a Tiered Prevention Framework

*Wendy Peia Oakes, Kathleen Lynne Lane, Eric Alan Common, and Mark Matthew Buckman*

## Abstract

Children and youth are experiencing emotional and behavioral disorders (EBD) in growing numbers, with recent cumulative rates indicating approximately 25% for those demonstrating impairment affecting their ability for successful academic, behavioral, and social development (Merikangas et al., 2010). The purpose of this paper is to present an overview of one tiered prevention framework—a comprehensive, integrated, three-tiered (Ci3T) model—for use within early childhood settings with a focus on systematic behavior screening for early detection of students who may require more intentional behavioral supports and instruction for school success. First, we present a tiered prevention framework for the promotion, prevention, and intervention of student learning in academic, behavioral, and social learning domains. Then we describe the use of universal behavior screening within tiered models of prevention for the early detection of students who may require additional supports. Third, we offer illustrations for using screening data along with other school-collected data for responding at Tiers 2 and 3 with practices that promote safe, positive learning environments for young students to gain skills and experiences according to their needs for school success. We conclude with a summary and direction for future inquiry to examined practices to prevent the development of learning and behavior challenges.

Keywords: Early childhood pre-K–Grade 3, emotional and behavioral disorders, systematic behavior screening, tiered prevention

# Introduction

Emotional and behavioral disorders (EBD) in young children are increasing in prevalence and magnitude, yet numbers for children receiving mental health supports or services remain very low (Child Mind Institute, 2015). Merikangas et al.'s (2010, 2011) findings from a national sample of U.S. youth ($N = 10,123$) captured the magnitude of the problem: 49.5% of youth manifested signs of EBD prior to age 18, and 27.6% experienced severe impairment; however, only slightly more than 33% accessed mental health supports. Youth experiencing anxiety disorders (e.g., generalized, separation, or social anxiety; phobias; panic disorders; and post-traumatic stress disorder [PTSD]) accessed services at even lower rates (fewer than 20%; Merikangas et al., 2011). This datum is important for all educators, as 80% of those who experience EBD in their lifetime undergo onset prior to age 18 (Forness, Freeman, Paparella, Kauffman, & Walker, 2012). Moreover, it is particularly relevant for early childhood educators, as anxiety disorders are not only the most prevalent EBD (31.9% of adolescents) but also have the earliest onset, at age six (Merikangas et al., 2010). These most recent prevalence rates demonstrate increases over those found a decade earlier when the U.S. Department of Health and Human Services (DHHS; 1999) reported 20% of children and youth were found to have experienced mild-to-severe EBD (also cumulative prevalence) with 10% found to have experienced severe EBD.

Early identification—such as through universal behavior screening practices—and intervention can prevent a host of negative outcomes associated with persistent EBD for children, their families, and their communities (Lane & Walker, 2015). In particular, teacher ratings of students' social and behavioral skills have been established as effective predictors of important outcomes for students (Oakes et al., 2010). For example, Jones, Greenberg, and Crowley (2015) found that teacher ratings of students' kindergarten prosocial skills were significant predictors 20 years later for deleterious outcomes (e.g., lower rates of high school graduation, unstable employment, need for public assistance). These patterns may begin when young students with mild and moderate forms of EBD experience difficult relationships with teachers and in turn may experience peer isolation, limited friendships and poor school learning experiences (McGrath & Van Bergen, 2015). Likewise, children experiencing severe EBD demonstrate limited involvement with family, school, and community activities (Brauner & Stephens, 2006). Without effective interventions implemented with fidelity, persistent EBD is associated with long-term outcomes such as academic failure, substance abuse, unemployment, and juvenile justice experience (Jones et al., 2015; McGrath & Van Bergen, 2015). Responding to findings, DHHS (1999) called for a response of promotion, prevention, and intervention efforts addressing social and emotional learning (SEL) in early childhood settings. A special report on child mental health recommended expanding research and use of reliable, valid screening measures, removing barriers to services, and the provision of a comprehensive system of interventions (Brauner & Stephens, 2006).

Tiered prevention models—such as positive behavior interventions and supports (PBIS; Horner & Sugai, 2015), the Teaching Pyramid Model (Fox, Dunlap, Hemmeter, Joseph, & Strain, 2003), and the comprehensive, integrated three-tiered (Ci3T) model of prevention (Lane, Kalberg, & Menzies, 2009)—provide frameworks for responding to these recommendations at the system level. Such prevention frameworks are grounded in the provision of safe and positive learning environments that promote and respond to students' needs across all learning domains including a strong focus on students' SEL. With use of a prevention framework, school systems are taking the responsibility for promotion and prevention practices, early identification of students experiencing or at risk for EBD through universal behavior screening, and a systemic response to students demonstrating needs beyond primary prevention (Tier 1 or universal) efforts. When these practices are implemented with fidelity, schools may also offer support to families of children with EBD who are in need of supports or services. Systematic behavior screening practices detect students with needs that may be addressed within the school context or by outside providers in partnership with the school (Lane, Oakes, Crocker, & Weist, 2017). Specifically, early childhood educators (pre-K–Grade 3) have a unique opportunity to affect a more positive trajectory for students by creating safe, positive, and proactive learning environments where teachers engage students with positive relationships and partner with families to support the development of prosocial skill sets. This systems-level approach in the school setting holds many benefits, particularly for families of children with or at risk for EBD who may not be familiar with how to best negotiate the challenging task of accessing needed supports (Brauner & Stephens, 2006).

## Purpose

The purpose of this paper is to present an overview of Ci3T within early childhood settings and the provision of systematic behavior screening within a Ci3T prevention framework for the early detection of students who may require more intentional behavioral supports and instruction. Specifically, we begin by describing the Ci3T framework for the promotion, prevention, and intervention in academic, behavioral, and social learning domains. Then we describe the use of universal behavior screening within tiered models of prevention for early detection of students who may require more intentional behavioral supports and instruction. Third, we offer illustrations for using screening data along with other school data to respond at Tiers 2 and 3 with practices that promote safe, positive learning environments for young students to gain skills and experiences according to their needs for school success. We conclude with a summary and direction for future inquiry to examine practices to prevent the development of learning and behavior challenges. While we frame these considerations within one tiered prevention framework, systematic behavior screening practices may be used within other frameworks as long as procedures are in place to respond to student needs when detected (Oakes, Lane, Cox, & Messenger, 2014).

## Comprehensive, Integrated, Three-tiered (Ci3T) Model of Prevention: A Focus on Early Childhood Contexts

The Ci3T model of prevention is a tiered system designed to meet pre-K–12 students' academic, behavioral, and social-emotional needs in a resource-efficient, collaborative manner (Lane, Oakes, Cantwell, & Royer, 2016). As with other tiered models, the cascade of supports increases in intensity according to student need, with primary prevention (Tier 1) efforts designed to promote development for all learners, secondary prevention (Tier 2) efforts designed for some students, and tertiary prevention (Tier 3) supports reserved for students with the most intensive intervention needs. In a Ci3T model, attention is focused on meeting students' multiple needs in a data-informed, integrated fashion at each level of prevention. For example, at Tier 1, in addition to receiving developmentally-appropriate instruction in alignment with the Council for Exceptional Children-Division of Early Childhood Recommended Practices (DEC; 2014) and early learning standards, students receive instruction in school-wide expectations operationalized for each setting (Royer, 2017; see Figure 1) and school-wide instruction in social skills using validated curricula, strategies, and practices (e.g., The Incredible Years Classroom Dinosaur Curriculum; Webster-Stratton, 2011). By creating a context in which all students receive opportunities to learn and practice prosocial skills which become the foundation for soft skills that support self-determined behaviors in an integrated fashion, students have hundreds of opportunities each day for positive interactions with adults and peers to build fluency in these skill sets (McGrath & Van Bergen, 2015). Developing early academic skills in tandem with behavioral and social skills, learners acquire a comprehensive repertoire of skills that facilitate positive, productive learning environments and empower them to build strong interpersonal relationships with teachers, family members, and peers (McIntosh & Goodman, 2015).

In the Ci3T model, several types of data are collected to inform decision making. For example, treatment-integrity data are collected in fall and spring of each academic year to ensure the Ci3T plan is implemented as designed (Gresham, 1989), as well as social-validity data to obtain stakeholders' views about the goals, procedures, and outcomes (Common & Lane, 2017; Wolf, 1978). At the student level, academic screening of early literacy and numeracy skills (e.g., AIMSweb, Pearson Education, 2008; Phonological Awareness Literacy Screening [PALS], Invernizzi, Sullivan, Meier, & Swank, 2004) and behavior screening tools (e.g., Systematic Screening for Behavior Disorders-Second Edition [SSBD], Walker, Severson, & Feil, 2014) are completed three times per year to benchmark students' performance as a baseline for monitoring those with low, moderate, and high levels of risk. Screening data along with other data collected as part of regular school practices, such as developmental screening (Ages and Stages Questionnaire—Social Emotional [ASQ-SE], Squires, Bricker, & Twombly, 2015) and progress data (e.g., Teaching Strategies GOLD, 2017) are analyzed in tandem to (a) examine the overall level of performance in a school or program, (b) inform the use of low-intensity, teacher-delivered strategies (e.g., active supervision, instructional choice), and (c) respond with validated Tier 2 and 3 supports when primary prevention efforts are not robust enough to meet students' needs.

As part of the Ci3T model, school leadership teams build a Ci3T Implementation Manual that includes a number of blueprints: Ci3T Blueprint A Primary (Tier 1) Plan, Ci3T Blueprint B Reactive Plan, Ci3T Blueprint C Expectation Matrix, Ci3T Blueprint D Assessment Schedule, Ci3T Blueprint E Secondary (Tier 2) Intervention Grid, and Ci3T Blueprint F Tertiary (Tier 3) Intervention Grid (see Ci3T. org/building). Each blueprint contains components that support implementation by ensuring transparency of all strategies, practices, and programs used in a school to support students' needs across academic, behavioral, and social domains. Additionally, the Ci3T Implementation Manual serves to focus professional learning efforts for developing the early childhood workforce (Lane et al., 2016). When designing a Ci3T model, school leadership teams make a number of critical decisions including the selection and adoption of academic and behavioral screening tools and a mapping-out of a focused professional learning plan. Ongoing professional learning offers time for school leadership, grade-level, and student services teams to review data (e.g., assess implementation, consider stakeholders' views of the Ci3T plan, and examine student performance) and make plans for addressing identified needs for continued improvement. Intentionality is needed for professional learning of specific research-based practices for early childhood educators.

## Practices to Promote High-Quality Learning Environments

Primary prevention efforts promote healthy development across all learning domains and relationship building across children, families, and colleagues to create a safe, positive, predictable, and proactive environment for student success. Primary prevention is predicated on positive relationships among children, families, and colleagues (Joseph & Strain, 2004). In turn, everyone is a productive developmental change agent empowered to facilitate children's development through effective teaching and guidance. The critical importance for promoting common features such as positive relationships and high-quality learning environments is well-established in the early childhood literature (Boyd et al., 2014).

In high-quality early learning environments, teachers (a) provide predictable schedules and routines, (b) plan the physical room arrangement to minimize areas that may contribute to difficulties (e.g., appropriate space to play, interact, and move between activities), and (c) support student engagement across a range of teacher- and student-led activities with optimal challenge within students' zones of proximal development (Simonsen, Fairbanks, Briesch, Myers, & Sugai, 2008). In addressing students' academic learning, teachers use core instructional programs according to early learning standard, providing a language- and print-rich environment, and developing learning centers with differentiated materials for number sense and literacy. Teachers also differentiate instruction (e.g., content, process, products), contextualize learning experiences, and foster students' curiosity in an effort to promote student engagement and foster intrinsic motivation (Lane, Menzies, Bruhn, & Cronbori, 2011).

## Practices to Promote Prosocial Behavior

An instructional approach is used to support all students in behaviors that facilitate learning and relationships. The National PBIS Center (OSEP-TAC; see pbis.org) and the National Center for Pyramid Model Innovations (NCPMI; see challengingbehavior.org) provide specific guidance for educators in designing the behavioral domain (e.g., PBIS) of the Ci3T model. For example, teachers display, teach, model, and reinforce expectations (see Figure 1 for example expectations matrix), and implement a reactive plan with fidelity. For example the reactive plan may include recognizing peers who are meeting expectations, redirecting students, re-teaching expectations, allowing students time to respond to the request and re-engage).

Additionally, a validated program addressing students' SEL supports foundational skills for all students, creating a school context that promotes prosocial behaviors. This includes targeting core competencies such as self-awareness, self-management, responsible decision making, relationship skills, and having social awareness (Collaborative for Academic, Social, and Emotional Learning [CASEL], 2005). Promoting SEL involves guiding young students to acquire and effectively apply the knowledge and skills to understand and manage emotions, set and achieve positive goals, feel and show empathy for others, establish and maintain positive relationships, and make responsible decisions (CASEL, 2013). These practices support students' development of self-regulation. As examples, teachers may provide multiple learning activities and opportunities for students to identify and name their own emotions. These activities develop the language of social interactions, empathy for others (Joseph, Strain, & Ostrosky, 2006), and provide a foundation for managing strong feelings (Webster-Stratton & Reid, 2004). The Incredible Years Dinosaur Curriculum (Webster-Stratton, 2011) is one example of a validated program that teachers and families of young students can use to promote SEL.

Positive guidance strategies (e.g., active supervision, instructional choice, high-probability request sequences, pre-correction) are daily teacher practices optimally integrated throughout primary prevention instruction across learning domains. For example, to facilitate students successfully navigating the classroom and difficult transitions, teachers may use pre-correction with active supervision to anticipate challenges and provide additional guidance, redirection, or feedback (National Center on Early Childhood Health and Wellness, n.d.). To increase student motivation and minimize non-compliance, teachers plan activities offering students instructional choices, such as learning center materials, order of activities, or options to practice or demonstrate skills (Conroy, Sutherland, Vo, Carr, & Ogston, 2014).

## Summary

High-quality learning environments provide for the promotion of academic, behavioral, and social learning and development. Through the use of primary prevention practices (Tier 1), young students are taught skills foundational to all learning and later school success such as building relationships with teachers and peers, listening and following directions, and accessing academic instruction with initiative and persistence. Primary prevention practices provide the strong foundational learning context; however, they are not expected to sufficiently meet the needs of all learners. Systematic screening provides a transparent process for early detection of those who may benefit from and require more intensive interventions.

## Universal Behavior Screening for Young Students within Tiered Models of Prevention

Systematic screening is a core feature for early detection of young students experiencing or at risk for EBD. Thus, it is a core practice in a Ci3T model of prevention. There are various types of screening tools, including developmental screeners (e.g., ASQ-SE, Squires et al., 2015), as well as behavior screeners—the focus of this article—for use with young students. Developmental screeners are often used within preschool settings for early detection of children with developmental delays or other disabilities as part of Child Find initiatives related to the Individuals with Disabilities Education Act (IDEA, 2004; The Early Childhood Technical Assistance Center [ECTA]). However, less attention has been devoted to understanding, adopting, and installing behavior screenings as part of regular school practices.

In general, behavior screenings are completed three times per year (fall, winter, and spring) by teachers and parents to benchmark socio-behavioral performance with a goal of detecting challenges at the earliest juncture, when behavior patterns are most amenable to intervention (Lane & Walker, 2015). The decision-making process for adopting and installing screening tools is driven by a number of considerations, such as the population of interest, reliability and validity of scores generated, associated time and personnel costs, financial costs, and functional utility of the tools for informing intervention efforts (Lane, Menzies, Oakes, & Kalberg, 2012). Below we provide a brief overview of four currently available screening tools to help inform the decision-making process in early childhood settings. We list these tools in alphabetical order and provide a brief description of each.

## Behavioral Assessment System for Children, Third Edition—Behavioral and Emotional Screening System (BASC-3 BESS)

The BASC-3 BESS (Kamphaus & Reynolds, 2015) is a commercially available screening tool for use with children and youth ages three to 18. It is offered in two versions: Preschool (ages 3–5) and Child/Adolescent (grades K–12). The BESS measures risk for EBD according to the following dimensions: externalizing problems, internalizing problems, school problems, and adaptive functioning (Dever, Mays, Kamphaus, & Dowdy, 2012). There are multi-informant measures for teachers, parents, and students (self-report, grades 3–12). Parent informant information may augment teacher ratings. However, DiStefano, Greer, and Dowdy (2017) found the BASC-3 BESS Parent-P Scale may underestimate preschool children's internalizing concerns. Therefore, relying on parent rating alone, for preschoolers, may not address concerns of delayed identification of students in need of services due to internalizing behavior challenges (Brauner & Stephens, 2006; DiStefano et al., 2017).

The measure is completed in full for each student prior to moving to the next student. Items (25–30) are rated on a 4-point Likert-type scale of *never, sometimes, often,* and *almost always* (some items are reflected for scoring). One overall score addresses the risk indices reported previously. Raw scores, percentiles, and risk classifications are available for interpretation. Risk classifications are calculated according to *t*-scores ($M = 50$, $SD = 10$): *normal* (0–60), *elevated* (61–70), or *extremely elevated* (71 or higher). The BESS demonstrates strong psychometric evidence with internal consistency correlations of .84 and a 3-week test-retest reliability of .81 for the teacher-completed version (Kamphaus & Reynolds, 2015).

The BESS takes approximately 5–10 min per student to complete. A variety of options are available for administration and scoring: Scantron forms scored using software with scanning and hand-entry options, online direct entry with seamless scoring and reporting system from Q-Global Pearson Education, and paper versions with hand or online entry with a range of related costs. Costs range from $60 (for paper administrations and unlimited online scoring per year and user) to $404 for a comprehensive kit with screening administration, scoring, and intervention recommendations. The complete BASC-3 system provides materials for assessment (screening, comprehensive assessment, direct observation protocols, developmental histories, and FLEX progress monitoring beginning at age 2, Reynolds & Kamphaus, 2016) and intervention materials for use classwide and for addressing students' Tier 2 and Tier 3 needs. It also offers Parent Tip Sheets for home-based use (BASC-3 Intervention Guide; Vannest, Reynolds, & Kamphaus, 2015). Professional learning is available, free of additional charge, from the publishers through online webinars; however, no training is needed to complete the BESS.

## Social Skills Improvement System—Social–emotional Learning Edition (SSiS-SEL)

The SSiS-SEL (Elliott & Gresham, 2017a) is a commercially available screening and progress monitoring tool for use with children ages 3 through Grade 8. This extension of the SSiS-Performance Screening Guide (Gresham & Elliott, 2007) provides additional information related to students' SEL. The original Prosocial scale was expanded to include five subscales corresponding with the theoretical model proposed by CASEL as a framework of social and emotional development of children (Elliott, Davies, Frey, Gresham, & Cooper, 2017). SSiS-SEL offers forms for multiple informants with teacher, parent, and child (self-report, beginning at age 8) versions available in English and Spanish.

The SSiS-SEL has eight subscales as follows: self-awareness, self-management, social awareness, relationship skills, responsible decision making, motivation to learn, reading skills, and mathematics skills. Teachers rate students according to five performance levels (5 = highest, green band to 1 = lowest, red band) descriptions, each with a set of behaviors characteristic of the subscale. Respondents select the level or band that best describes the student's current performance. All students in a class are rated on each subscale before moving to the next. For interpretation, scores of 1 or 2 on any subscale indication potential risk in need of intervention. Two composite scores are also calculated, with the first five items representing the social-emotional (SE) score and the remaining three comprising the academic functioning (AF) score. Composite scores are interpreted thus: SE scores ≤ 10 indicates "at risk" and AF scores ≤ 6 indicates "at risk." The SSiS-SEL has strong psychometric evidence supporting valid and reliable scores (Elliott et al., 2017). The measure shows strong content validity applying the CASEL framework of SEL competencies. Reliability is demonstrated by high internal consistency alphas (total scale .93; SE = .91, AF = .91) and test–retest correlations over a 1-month period (SE = .887, AF = .910).

SSiS-SEL requires 30–45 min for a teacher to screen a class of students and can be completed online or using paper copies (available from Pearson PsychCorp). The financial investment ranges from $55 for a one-year subscription for scoring per user, to $534 for a comprehensive screening and intervention package for multiple informants in English and Spanish, per year per user. A range of options is available to meet desired school needs. The SSiS is a family of tools offering one comprehensive system to assess (screening, rating scales, and progress monitoring) and intervene (Classwide Intervention Program [CIP], Elliott & Gresham, 2017b). The CIP is designed for use at all three tiers of promotion, prevention, and responding and is deemed by CASEL to be an evidence-based treatment (DiPerna, Lei, Cheng, Hart, & Bellinger, 2017). Lessons correspond with skills identified on the SSiS-SEL for a seamless assessment and intervention package. Professional learning is available, free of additional charge, from the publishers through online webinars.

## Strengths and Difficulties Questionnaire (SDQ)

The SDQ (Goodman, 2001) is a free-access behavior screening tool for use with students ages 2–17 in three age-range versions: 2–4, 4–10, and 11–17. The SDQ assesses five domains of development with the following subscales: emotional symptoms, conduct problems, hyperactivity, peer relationship problems, and prosocial behavior. Items (25) are scored using a 3-point Likert-type scale where 0 = *not true*, 1 = *somewhat true*, and 2 = *certainly true*, evaluating the occurrence of each behavior during the last six months or current school year. Scores for the first four domains are summed for a total difficulties score. Four-band risk categories are established for domains and total difficulties score: *close to average, slightly raised, high*, and *very high* (Youth in Mind, 2015). Scales are available for multiple informants, teachers, parents and the student (self-report, beginning at age 11) and in multiple languages.

The SDQ is available online and can be downloaded for printing if needed. Scoring can be done through a variety of statistical programs (SPSS, SAS, Stata and R syntax available from the publisher, www.sdqinfo.org), online through the website, or through hand scoring. Reports vary depending on the scoring form selected. Scoring time and accuracy is improved when using online or statistical programming. The SDQ has a wealth of evidence demonstrating reliability and validity across time and contexts. The teacher version demonstrates reliability with alpha coefficients ranging from .70 (peer problems) to .88 (hyperactivity), and .87 for Total Difficulties (Goodman, 2001). Concurrent validity was established with the Child Behavior Checklist (Achenbach, 1991), a well-established comprehensive measure of children's behavioral development.

When using the English (USA) version, completion time is approximately 30 min per student. The total scale is completed for each student before moving on to the next student. Reports are produced for each student separately. One factor for consideration is the amount of time needed for teachers or school personnel to aggregate the data for monitoring school- or program-level shifts in risk (Lane et al., 2012). While the SDQ is free to access, there are potential financial considerations: access to computers for each teacher; access to paper for making copies (one page per student per screening time point); and the above-mentioned cost in personnel time. The SDQ is a stand-alone screening tool. School leadership teams would select and develop intervention responses for addressing children's needs at Tier 2 and Tier 3. The measure offers a viable tool for screening children in early childhood settings, particularly for those with limited financial resources to invest in screening.

## Systematic Screening for Behavior Disorders, Second Edition (SSBD)

The SSBD (Walker et al., 2014) is a commercially available tool for use in grades pre-K–9. It identifies students at risk for the two major categories of childhood mental health disorders, internalizing and externalizing. The SSBD is a teacher-completed multiple-gating screening tool. In stage 1, teachers consider the behavioral patterns of all students in their class and then nominate the five students in each category—internalizing and externalizing—whose behaviors most closely match the provided definitions (which include behavioral examples and non-examples). Once five students are listed in each category, teachers rank students on each list, from most to least like the definition. In stage 2, teachers rate the three highest ranked students in each category using rating scales— Critical Events Index (there are 33 critical events; e.g., sets fires) and Combined Frequency Index of Adaptive and Maladaptive Behavior (23 items [11 maladaptive, 12 adaptive]) using a 5-point Likert-type scale (1 = *never* to 5 = *frequently*). Children who exceed normative criteria are then considered for Tier 2 or 3 intervention or supports. Norms were updated in 2013 based on a nationally representative sample of over 7,000 students (Walker et al., 2014). At stage 3, teachers may elect to use the direct observation protocol (Screening, Identification, and Monitoring System [SIMS] Behavior

Observation Codes) and conduct a records review (School Archival Records Search [SARS]). Stage 3 efforts may inform a comprehensive response accessing school and community-based providers (Lane et al., 2017). SSBD, 2nd edition was revised to better address considerations at the preschool level. These revisions resulted in one screening measure for pre-K–Grade 9, integrating the previous early-childhood-focused Early Screening Project (Walker, Severson, & Feil, 1995) into the SSBD, 2nd edition.

The SSBD is available to schools in online and in paper formats for selection depending on available resources. While online scoring may be preferred for increased efficiency and accuracy, paper scoring takes little training. Often considered the 'gold standard' in screening, the SSBD has strong reliability and validity. Reliability item-total correlations were .94 (adaptive behavior) to .92 (maladaptive behavior). Multiple measures of validity support the use of the SSBD (Walker et al., 2014).

Stages 1 and 2 take about 40 minutes per class to complete. Reports are provided with online scoring; otherwise, personnel time is needed for aggregating scores for classrooms, grade levels, and for school- or program-level interpretations (Lane et al., 2012). The SSBD ranges in cost depending on system selected—the portfolio (administrator guide, technical manual, 10 screening packets grades 1–9, two screening packets grades pre-K–K) costs $225, with additional screening packets available at $10 per classroom. The online option costs about $30 per 100 students (www.pacificnwpublish.com). For early childhood settings, the SSBD coordinates with *First Step Next* (Walker et al., 2015), an updated version of *First Step to Success*, an evidence-based Tier 2 program with positive effects for children's emotional/internal behavior, external behavior, and social outcomes (What Works Clearinghouse, 2012). School leadership teams would also select and develop intervention responses for addressing children's needs at Tier 2 and Tier 3.

## Summary

The foregoing describes four options for early childhood educators to use for early detection of children experiencing or at risk for EBD. Each was selected for its strong psychometric evidence, feasible application in schools, and useful information for making instructional decisions regarding school-wide practices as well as individual students who may benefit from more targeted (Tier 2) or intensive (Tier 3) supports. In the next section, we offer a few illustrations of validated Tier 2 and Tier 3 supports for young children requiring assistance beyond primary prevention efforts.

## Using Systematic Screening Data for Tiered Supports

When Tier 1 is implemented with integrity, and positive guidance strategies such as active supervision and pre-correction are regularly implemented as part of promotion and prevention practices, the student data support decisions for more intensive intervention efforts. In a Ci3T model of prevention, school leadership teams consider multiple sources of data, as previously described; select the appropriate support or validated curricula; and ensure professional learning is available, as needed, for high fidelity implementation. Secondary prevention (Tier 2) efforts may be more intentional or target use of positive guidance strategies or instruction for specific skill development. Tertiary prevention (Tier 3) is for responding to students' most intensive needs through the use of individualized instruction or supports. School Ci3T leadership teams list all available Tier 2 and 3 supports and strategies in the school's Ci3T Implementation Manual. They are listed in the Ci3T Blueprint E Secondary (Tier 2; see example in Figure 2) Intervention Grid and Ci3T Blueprint E Tertiary (Tier 3; see Figure 3) Intervention Grid. Having the strategies listed in the manual allows for transparency of the full range of available supports (see Figures 2 and 3 for examples). Intervention Grids facilitate efficient decision-making with the following information: (a) intervention name and description, and three data-based decision guidance:

(b) entry criteria, (c) progress monitoring, and (d) exit criteria (Lane et al., 2016).

## Responding at Tier 2

Tier 2 supports and interventions are most often integrated within the classroom schedule and routines, and can be implemented by classroom teachers and staff. Tier 2 supports may include intentional individual use of promotion strategies (such as using pre-correction for individual students, followed by higher rates of behavior-specific praise when expectations are met); individualized schedules manipulated by students as they progress through the day (Hemmeter, Ostrosky, & Corso, 2012); specific strategies used by teachers to support transitioning, such as engaging the student in a less-preferred "buffer" activity prior to the call for transition (Lawry, Danko, & Strain, 2000); and the use of social stories to provide individualized instruction for a specific social skill (Schneider & Goldstein, 2010).

Similar to the responses for addressing academic learning needs—additional instruction and practice with feedback—students experiencing higher levels of behavior or social-skill needs, as detected on behavior screening tools, may benefit from additional instruction, practice, and feedback in these domains. For example, early childhood teachers may use a validated curriculum such as the Incredible Years Classroom Dinosaur Program for all students as part of Tier 1. Then, for students who require additional instruction, teachers may implement the Small Group Dinosaur Program (Webster-Stratton, 2013) available as a companion to the classroom program (i.e., Tier 2). This program provides curricula for two hours of weekly instruction for 18–22 weeks, allowing students additional targeted practice with important skills (e.g., problem solving, making and maintaining friendships, and skills that facilitate positive school experiences [e.g., following directions, asking for help, learning school rules]). As would be expected in early childhood settings, a home component is included to promote the learning of these important social skills across contexts. Having the Tier 2 intervention as an extension of Tier 1 allows for language systems and skills to be consistent, with a higher likelihood that they will be supported across classroom, school, and home contexts.

Established, data-based entry criteria are used for determining the most appropriate intervention for a student. Criteria are built on data collected as part of the Tier 1 plan (e.g., universal screening data, academic screening and progress data, attendances). Then progress is more frequently monitored for the targeted skills. Progress-monitoring tools may be included in specific curricula, as a companion tool to the universal screener used at Tier 1 (e.g., FLEX, Kamphaus & Reynolds, 2015), or a more universal tool to monitor frequent progress (e.g., Electronic Daily Behavior Report Card; Vannest, Burke, & Adiguzel, 2006). Finally, exit criteria are used for determining when the intervention or support may be ended, faded, or a different intervention recommended, either another Tier 2 or more intensive Tier 3 support. For the few students demonstrating the most intensive needs, or those who may be exposed to multiple risk factors, Tier 3 supports or interventions are available.

## Responding at Tier 3

Tier 3 interventions have an explicit, individualized focus on remediation of skills (Harn, Kame'enui, & Simmons, 2007). Where available, Tier 3 supports may be supported by school or district specialists or instructional coaches. These specialists often have expertise to help teachers select the most appropriate intervention and provide support for high fidelity implementation and data collection. For example, functional assessment-based interventions (FABI) are a promising practice to address severe challenging behaviors of young children (Wood, Oakes, Fettig, & Lane, 2015) and school-aged students more broadly (What Works Clearinghouse, 2016).

Umbreit, Ferro, Liaupsin, and Lane (2007) developed a systematic approach to identifying maintaining function(s), or purpose, of target behaviors and designing interventions linked to results of the functional assessment. The FABI model facilitates direct use of functional behavioral assessment (FBA) data in developing an individualized behavior intervention plan (BIP; see Ci3T.org/fabi). FABIs are based on the reasons why challenging behavior occurs (function). A *Function Matrix* supports the organization of the FBA data for making a data-informed hypothesis statement. *The Function-Based Intervention Decision Model* guides the determination of the intervention focus: Method 1: teach the replacement behavior; Method 2: improve the environment; Method 3: adjust the contingencies; and a combination of Method 1 and Method 2 (Umbreit et al., 2007). An individualized BIP is then designed and implemented. Interventions address needed antecedent adjustments, reinforcement adjustments, and extinction procedures (or A-R-E components) which are directly linked back to the function of the target (problem) behavior.

## Summary

Tier 2 and 3 supports are additive in nature, meaning they are supplemental to Tier 1 and do not replace Tier 1 instruction (Balu et al., 2015). Students participating in a tiered intervention or support may continue to benefit from Tier 1 for the promotion of positive learning outcomes. When tiered supports are directly connected to Tier 1 practices, they are most likely to be reinforced in the classroom context by both peers and adults. Tier 3 supports, such as FABI, are appropriate for students exposed to multiple risk factors (Patterson, DeBaryshe, & Ramsey, 1989), as well as those for whom primary and secondary (Tier 2) efforts alone have not yet yielded desired shifts in performance or development, and may be considered for those showing the highest risk according to the selected screening tool.

## A Call for Action: Considerations for Future Inquiry

As educational systems recognize and take responsibility for the prevention of EBD, early childhood educators have the unique opportunity for the promotion of healthy development across all learning domains in partnerships with students' families (DEC, 2014). Tiered models of prevention with the provision of universal systematic screening practices align with the call to action by DHH (1999) and the recommendations of a special report on public health for the use of reliable and valid screening measures, removing barriers to services, and the provision of a comprehensive system of interventions (Brauner & Stephens, 2006).

Early childhood educators, their students, and the students' families may benefit from continued inquiry into the adoption of tiered models of prevention in early childhood settings, as well as the use of screening practices for early detection of students in need of more intensive supports. Moreover, it is essential to examine important learning outcomes of students across academic, behavioral, and social domains who attend schools that implement such models. Further, research on the promotion of practices with high-fidelity implementation would continue to inform professional development and teacher preparation efforts as we work as a field to develop a highly effective educational workforce (Lane et al., 2016). We look forward to learning from highly committed practitioners and scholars who continue to explore these important lines of inquiry.

**Author's Note:** For inquiries regarding this article, please contact Wendy Peia Oakes, Ph.D. Assistant Professor in the Mary Lou Fulton Teachers College, Arizona State University, P.O. Box 87-5411, Tempe, AZ 85287-5411, wendy.oakes@asu.edu.

## References

Achenbach, T. M. (1991). *Integrative guide for the 1991 CBCL/4-18, YRS, & TRF profiles.* Burlington, VT: University of Vermont, Department of Psychiatry.

Balu, R., Zhu, P., Doolittle, F., Schiller, E., Jenkins, J., & Gersten, R. (2015). *Evaluation of response to intervention practices for elementary school reading.* Washington, D.C.: U.S. Department of Education, Institute of Education Sciences. Retrieved from http://ies.ed.gov/ncee

Boyd, B. A., Hume, K., McBee, M. T., Alessandri, M., Guitierrez, A., Johnson, L., ... Odom, S.L. (2014). Comparative efficacy of LEAP, TEACCH and non-model-specific special education programs for preschoolers with autism spectrum disorders. *Journal of Autism and Developmental Disorders, 44,* 366–380. doi:10.1007/ s10803-013-1877-9

Brauner, C. B., & Stephens, C. B. (2006). Estimating the prevalence of early childhood serious emotional/behavioral disorders: Challenges and recommendations. *Public Health Reports, 121,* 303–310.

Child Mind Institute. (2015). *Children's mental health report.* New York, NY: Author. Retrieved from https://childmind.org/our-impact/childrens-mental-health-report/

Collaborative for Academic, Social, and Emotional Learning. (2013). *2013 CASEL guide: Effective social and emotional learning programs—Preschool and elementary school edition.* Chicago, IL: Author. Retrieved from www.casel.org/

Collaborative for Academic, Social, and Emotional Learning (2005). *Social emotional learning (SEL) competencies.* Chicago, IL: Author. Retrieved from www.casel.org/

Common, E. A., & Lane, K. L. (2017). Social validity assessment. In J. K. Luiselli (Ed.), *Applied behavior analysis advanced guidebook: A manual for professional practice* (pp. 73–92). London: Elsevier. Manuscript in review.

Conroy, M. A., Sutherland, K. S., Vo, A. K., Carr, S., & Ogston, P. L. (2014). Early childhood teachers' use of effective instructional practices and the collateral effects on young children's behavior. *Journal of Positive Behavior Interventions, 16,* 81–92.

Dever, B. V., Mays, K. L., Kamphaus, R. W., & Dowdy, E. (2012). The factor structure of the BASC-2 behavioral and emotional screening system teacher form, child/adolescent. *Journal of Psychoeducational Assessment, 30,* 488–495. doi:10.1177/073428291243886

DiPerna, J., Lei, P., Cheng, W., Hart, S., & Bellinger, J. (2017). A cluster randomized trial of the Social Skills Improvement System-Classwide Intervention Program (SSIS-CIP) in first grade. *Journal of Educational Psychology.* http://dx.doi.org/10.1037/edu0000191

DiStefano, C., Greer, F. W., & Dowdy, E. (2017). Examining the BASC-3 BESS Parent Form–Preschool using Rasch methodology. *Assessment*. doi:10.1177/1073191117723112.

Division for Early Childhood. (2014). *DEC recommended practices in early intervention/ early childhood special education 2014*. Retrieved from http://www. dec-sped.org/recommendedpractices

Elliott, S. N., Davies, M. D., Frey, F. R., Gresham, F. & Cooper, G. (2017). Development and initial validation of the social emotional learning assessment for universal screening. *Journal of Applied Developmental Psychology*. Retrieved from http://dx.doi.org/10.1016/j.appdev.2017.06.002

Elliott, S. N., & Gresham, F. (2017a). *Social Skills Improvement System (SSiS)—Social Emotional Learning*. San Antonio, TX: PsychCorp Pearson Education.

Elliott, S. N., & Gresham, F. (2017b). *Social Skills Improvement System (SSiS)— Classwide Intervention Program*. San Antonio, TX: PsychCorp Pearson Education.

Forness, S. R., Freeman, S. F. N., Paparella, T., Kauffman, J. M., & Walker, H. M. (2012). Special education implications of point and cumulative prevalence for children with emotional or behavioral disorders. *Journal of Emotional and Behavioral Disorders, 20*, 4–18. doi:10.1177/1063426611401624

Fox, L., Dunlap, G., Hemmeter, M. L., Joseph, G. E., & Strain, P. S. (2003). The teaching pyramid: A model for supporting social competence and preventing challenging behavior in young children. *Young Children, 58*(4), 48–52.

Goodman, R. (2001). Psychometric properties of the Strengths and Difficulties Questionnaire (SDQ). *Journal of the American Academy of Child and Adolescent Psychiatry, 40*, 1337–1345. doi:10.1097/00004583-200111000-00015.

Gresham, F. M. (1989). Assessment of treatment integrity in school consultation and prereferral intervention. *School Psychology Review, 18*, 37–50.

Gresham, F. M., & Elliott, S. N. (2007). *Social skills improvement system: Performance screening guides*. Bloomington, MN: Pearson Assessments.

Harn, B. A., Kame'enui, E. J., & Simmons, D. C. (2007). Essential features of interventions for kindergarten students most in need of accelerated learning: The nature and role of the third tier in a prevention model for kindergarten students. In D. Haager, J. Klinger, & S. Vaughn (Eds.), *Evidence-based reading practices for response to intervention* (pp. 161–184). Baltimore, MD: Brookes.

Hemmeter, M. L., Ostrosky, M. M. & Corso, R. M. (2012). Preventing and addressing challenging behavior: Common questions and practical strategies. *Young Exceptional Children, 15*(2), 32–46.

Horner, R. H., & Sugai, G. (2015). School-wide PBIS: An example of applied behavior analysis implemented at a scale of social importance. *Behavior Analysis in Practice, 8*, 80–85. doi:10.1007/s40617-015-0045-4

Individuals with Disabilities Education Improvement Act of 2004, 20 U.S.C. 1400 *et seq.* (2004).

Invernizzi, M., Sullivan, A., Meier, J., & Swank, L. (2004). *Phonological Awareness Literacy Screening [PALS]: PreK Teacher's Manual.* Richmond, VA: University of Virginia

Jones, D. E., Greenberg, M., & Crowley, M. (2015). Early social–emotional functioning and public health: The relationship between kindergarten social competence and future wellness. *American Journal of Public Health, 105*, 2283–2290.

Joseph, G. E., Strain, P. S. (2004). Building positive relationships with young children. *Young Exceptional Children, 7*(4), 21–28.

Joseph, G. E., Strain, P., & Ostrosky, M. (2006). *What works brief 21: Fostering emotional literacy in young children: Labeling emotions.* Nashville, TN: Center on the Social and Emotional Foundations for Learning.

Kamphaus, R. W., & Reynolds, C. R. (2015). *Behavior Assessment System for Children-Third Edition (BASC-3): Behavioral and Emotional Screening System (BESS).* Bloomington, MN: Pearson.

Lane, K. L., Kalberg, J. R., & Menzies, H. M. (2009). *Developing schoolwide programs to prevent and manage problem behaviors: A step-by-step approach.* New York: Guilford.

Lane, K. L., Menzies, H. M., Bruhn, A. L., & Crnobori, M. E. (2011). *Managing challenging behaviors in schools: Research-based strategies that work.* New York: Guilford.

Lane, K. L., Menzies, H. M, Oakes, W. P., & Kalberg, J. R. (2012). *Systematic screenings of behavior to support instruction: From preschool to high school.* New York: Guilford.

Lane, K. L., Oakes, W. P., Cantwell, E. D., & Royer, D. J. (2016). *Building and installing comprehensive, integrated, three-tiered (Ci3T) models of prevention: A practical guide to supporting school success.* Phoenix, AZ: KOI Education. (Interactive eBook)

Lane, K. L., Oakes, W. P., Crocker, J., & Weist, M. D. (2017). Building strong partnerships: Education and mental health systems working together to advance behavioral health screening in schools. *Report on Emotional & Behavioral Disorders in Youth, 17*, 93–101.

Lane, K. L. & Walker, H. M. (2015). The connection between assessment and intervention: How does screening lead to better interventions? In B. Bateman, M. Tankersley, and J. Lloyd (Eds.). (pp. 283–301). *Enduring issues in special education: Personal perspectives.* New York, NY: Routledge.

Lawry, J., Danko, C. D., & Strain, P. S. (2000). Examining the role of the classroom environment in the prevention of problem behaviors. *Young Exceptional Children, 3*(2), 11–19.

McGrath, K. F., & Van Bergen, P. (2015). Who, when, why and to what end? Students at risk of negative student–teacher relationships and their outcomes. *Educational Research Review, 14*, 1–17. doi:org/10.1016/j.edurev.2014.12.001

McIntosh K., & Goodman, S. (2015). *Integrating multi-tiered systems of support: Blending RTI and PBIS.* New York, NY. Guilford Press.

Merikangas, K. R., Hep, J., Burstein, M., Swanson, S., Avenevoli, S., Cui, L., … Swendsen, J. (2010). Lifetime prevalence of mental disorders in U.S. adolescents: results from the National Comorbidity Survey Replication—Adolescent Supplement (NCS-A). *Journal of American Academy of Child and Adolescent Psychiatry, 49*, 980–989. doi:10.1016/j.jaac.2010.05.017

Merikangas, K. R, Jian-ping, H, Burstein, M. E., Swedensen, J., Avenevoli, S., Case, B. … Olfson, M. (2011). Service utilization for lifetime mental disorders in U.S. adolescents: results of the national comorbidity survey adolescent supplement (NCS-A). *Journal of American Academy of Child and Adolescent Psychiatry, 50*, 32–45. doi:10.1016/j.jaac.2010.10.006

National Center on Early Childhood Health and Wellness, (n.d.). *Active supervision.* Washington, DC: Author.

Oakes, W. P., Lane, K. L., Cox, M. L., & Messenger, M. (2014). Logistics of behavior screenings: How and why do we conduct behavior screenings at our school? *Preventing School Failure: Alternative Education for Children and Youth, 58*, 159–170. doi:10.1080/1045988X.2014.89557

Oakes, W. P., Wilder, K., Lane, K. L., Powers, L., Yokoyama, L., O'Hare, M. E., & Jenkins, A.B. (2010). Psychometric properties of the Student Risk Screening Scale: An effective tool for use in diverse urban elementary schools. *Assessment for Effective Intervention, 35*, 231–239.

Patterson, G. R., DeBaryshe, B. D., & Ramsey, E. (1989). A developmental perspective on antisocial behavior. *American Psychological Association, 44*, 329–335.

Pearson Education (2008). *AIMSweb.* San Antonio, TX: Author.

Reynolds, C. R., & Kamphaus, R. W. (2016). *Behavior Assessment System for Children-Third Edition (BASC-3): Flex Monitor.* Bloomington, MN: Pearson Education.

Royer, D. J. (2017). *Examining the utility of the School-wide Expectations Survey for Specific Settings (SESSS): A data-informed approach to developing expectation matrices* (Unpublished doctoral dissertation). University of Kansas, Lawrence, KS.

Schneider, N., & Goldstein, H. (2010). Using social stories and visual schedules to improve socially appropriate behaviors in children with autism. *Journal of Positive Behavior Interventions, 12,* 149–160. doi:10.1177/109830070933

Simonsen, B., Fairbanks, S., Briesch, A., Myers, D., & Sugai, G. (2008). Evidence-based practices in classroom management: Considerations for research to practice. *Education and Treatment of Children, 31,* 351–380. doi:10.1353/etc.0.0007

Squires, J., Bricker, D., & Twombly, E. (2015). *Ages and Stages Questionnaires—Social-emotional: A parent-completed child monitoring system for social–emotional behaviors* (2nd ed.). Baltimore, MD: Paul H. Brookes Publishing.

Teaching Strategies GOLD (2017). *GOLD.* Bethesda, MD: Teaching Strategies LLC.

Umbreit, J., Ferro, J., Liaupsin, C., & Lane, K. (2007). *Functional behavioral assessment and function-based intervention: An effective, practical approach.* Upper Saddle River, NJ: Prentice-Hall.

U.S. Department of Health and Human Services (1999). *Mental health: a report of the Surgeon General.* Rockville, MD: Author.

Vannest, K. J., Burke, M. D, & Adiguzel, T. (2006). Electronic Daily Behavior Report Card (e-DBRC): A web based system for progress monitoring (Version 3.0) [Web-based application]. College Station, TX: Texas A&M University. Retrieved from http://d2k.tamu.edu/products/e-dbrc.php

Vannest, K. J., Reynolds, C. R., & Kamphaus, R. (2015). *Behavior Assessment System for Children-Third Edition (BASC-3): Intervention guide & materials.* Bloomington, MN: Pearson.

Walker, H. M., Severson, H. H., & Feil, E. G. (1995). *Early screening project.* Eugene, OR: Pacific Northwest Publishing.

Walker, H. M., Severson, H. H., & Feil, E. G. (2014). *Systematic screening for behavior disorders (SSBD) technical manual: Universal screening for pre-K–9* (2nd ed.). Eugene, OR: Pacific Northwest Publishing.

Walker, H., Stiller, B., Coughlin, C., Golly, A., Sprick, M., & Feil, E. (2015) *First Step Next.* Eugene, OR: Pacific Northwest Publishing.

Webster-Stratton, C. (2011). *Incredible Years.* Seattle, WA: The Incredible Years.

Webster-Stratton, C. (2013). *Dina dinosaur's social skills and problem solving curriculum for the classroom.* Seattle, WA: The Incredible Years.

Webster-Stratton, C., & Reid, M. J. (2004). Strengthening social and emotional competence in young children—the foundation for early school readiness and success: Incredible Years Classroom Social Skills and Problem-solving Curriculum. *Infants & Young Children, 17,* 96–113.

What Works Clearinghouse, U.S. Department of Education, Institute of Education Sciences (2012). *WWC Intervention Report: Children classified as having emotional disturbance: First Step to Success.* Washington, DC: Author.

What Works Clearinghouse, U.S. Department of Education, Institute of Education Sciences (2016). *WWC Intervention Report: Children classified as having emotional disturbance: Functional behavioral assessment-based interventions.* Washington, DC: Author.

Witt, J.C. & Elliott, S.N. (1985). Acceptability of classroom intervention strategies. In Kratochwill, T.R. (Ed.), *Advances in school psychology,* Vol. 4, 251–288. Mahwah, NJ: Erlbaum.

Wolf, M. M. (1978). Social validity: The case for subjective measurement or how applied behavior analysis is finding its heart. *Journal of Applied Behavior Analysis, 11,* 203–214.

Wood, B. K., Oakes, W. P., Fettig, A., & Lane, K. L. (2015). A review of the evidence base of functional assessment-based interventions for young students using one systematic approach. *Behavioral Disorders, 40,* 230–250.

Youth in Mind (2015). *Scoring the SDQ.* Retrieved from http://www.sdqinfo.com/py/sdqinfo/c0.py

**Figure 1.**
***Early childhood expectations matrix***

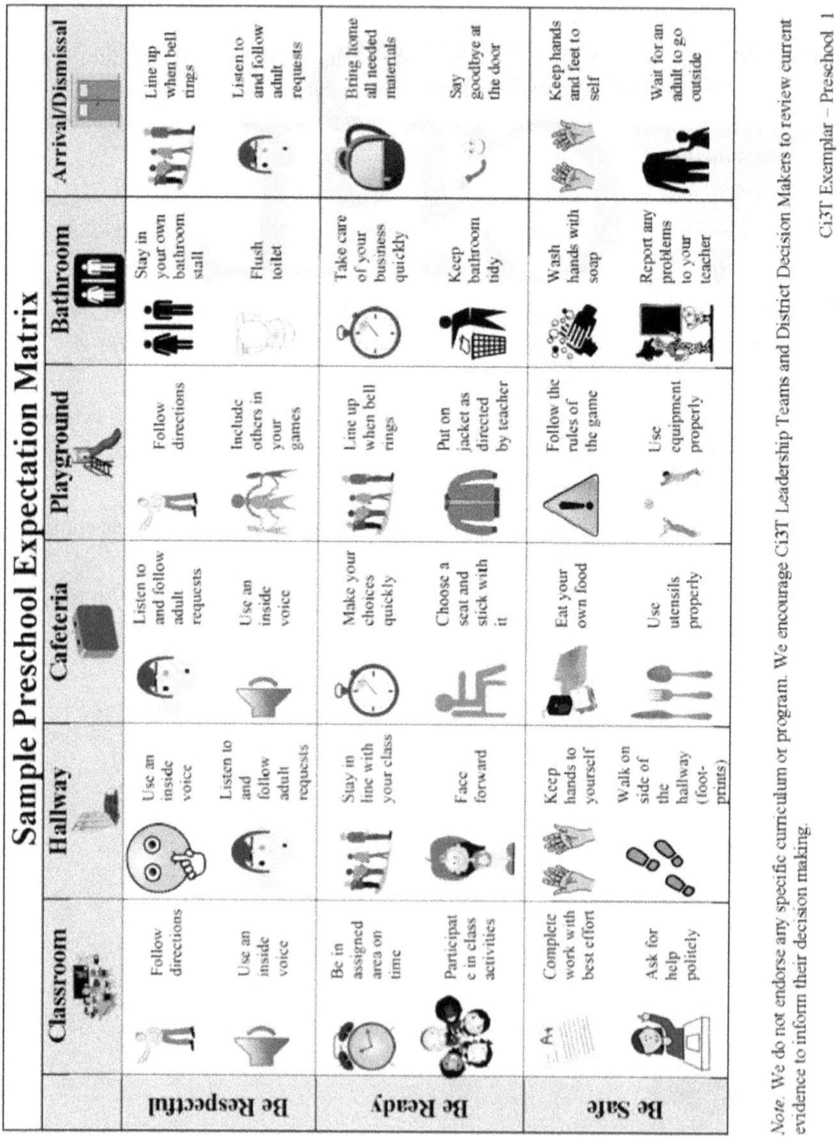

Sample Preschool Expectation Matrix

| | Classroom | Hallway | Cafeteria | Playground | Bathroom | Arrival/Dismissal |
|---|---|---|---|---|---|---|
| Be Respectful | Follow directions<br>Use an inside voice | Use an inside voice<br>Listen to and follow adult requests | Listen to and follow adult requests<br>Use an inside voice | Follow directions<br>Include others in your games | Stay in your own bathroom stall<br>Flush toilet | Line up when bell rings<br>Listen to and follow adult requests |
| Be Ready | Be in assigned area on time<br>Participat e in class activities | Stay in line with your class<br>Face forward | Make your choices quickly<br>Choose a seat and stick with it | Line up when bell rings<br>Put on jacket as directed by teacher | Take care of your business quickly<br>Keep bathroom tidy | Bring home all needed materials<br>Say goodbye at the door |
| Be Safe | Complete work with best effort<br>Ask for help politely | Keep hands to yourself<br>Walk on side of the hallway (foot-prints) | Eat your own food<br>Use utensils properly | Follow the rules of the game<br>Use equipment properly | Wash hands with soap<br>Report any problems to your teacher | Keep hands and feet to self<br>Wait for an adult to go outside |

*Note.* We do not endorse any specific curriculum or program. We encourage Ci3T Leadership Teams and District Decision Makers to review current evidence to inform their decision making.

Ci3T Exemplar – Preschool 1

*From Lane, Oakes, Cantwell, & Royer (2016).* Building and installing comprehensive, integrated, three-tiered (Ci3T) models of prevention: A practical guide to supporting school success. *Phoenix, AZ: KOI Education. © 2017 Authors. Reproduced with permission.*

**Figure 2.**
*Tier 2 Intervention Grid with an example intervention at the early childhood level*

| Support | Description | School-wide data: entry criteria | Data to monitor progress | Exit criteria |
|---|---|---|---|---|
| Small Group Dinosaur Program (Webster-Stratton, 2013) | Table Components: Small group instruction in the classroom, weekly two hours for 18–22 weeks. Instruction and practice for targeted SEL skills: problem solving, making and maintaining friendships, and skills that facilitate positive school experiences such as following directions, asking for help, learning school rules.<br><br>Family component: Letters sent to parents with personal contact about program prior to beginning, then weekly contact with teacher. Shared behaviors are selected for monitoring. Parents contribute examples for problem solving lessons at school (specific real scenarios). Regular home activities—contact prior to sending each home. Home activities may be written or digitally recorded. | SSBD score exceeding normative criteria for internalizing or externalizing scales. | Electronic Daily Behavior Report Card of skills learning in the small group.<br><br>Treatment integrity of intervention and dosage.<br><br>Social validity surveys for parents and students. | SSBD scores below criteria for identification of risk.<br><br>Completion of curriculum.<br><br>Review of progress and feedback from family. |

*Note. SSBD = Systematic Screener for Behavioral Disorders (Walker, Severson, & Feil, 2014).*

## Figure 3.
### *Tier 3 Intervention Grid with an example intervention at the early childhood level*

| Support | Description | School-wide data: entry criteria | Data to monitor progress | Exit criteria |
|---|---|---|---|---|
| Functional Assessment-based Intervention (FABI) | FABIs are interventions based on the function of the target behavior. (1) Student is identified for FABI. (2) Information is collected as part of functional assessment (e.g., review of student records; teacher, parent, and student interviews; direct observation; rating scales) to identify target behavior and its function as determined by the functional assessment and determined with the aid of the *Function Matrix*. A replacement behavior is operationalized. (3) Baseline data is collected to determine present levels or target and/or replacement behavior. (4) An intervention is designed (Behavior Intervention Plan [BIP]) using *The Function-Based Intervention Decision Model* to determine the intervention focus, including: Method 1: Teach the replacement behavior; Method 2: Improve the environment; Method 3: Adjust the contingencies; and a combination of Method 1 and Method 2. A package intervention is designed and implemented, including antecedent (A-) adjustments, reinforcement (R-) adjustments, and extinction (E) procedures directly linked to the function of the target behavior. (5) Procedural fidelity, social validity and student outcome data are collected and assessed to determine the effects of the intervention. | One or more of the following: -BASC-3 BESS – extremely elevated risk (71 or higher) across one or more subscales: externalizing problems, internalizing problems, school problems, and adaptive functioning -Previously participated in secondary interventions used between screenings with documentation of lack of success for academic and behavioral performance | **Student performance** Student behavior targeted for improvement (e.g., target or replacement behavior) using behavior measurement system (e.g., duration, frequency, interval recording) •Graphing of data to etermine changes in behavior across conditions (e.g., baseline, intervention, withdrawal, reintroduction) **Treatment integrity** •FABI Step Checklists •A-R-E component treatment integrity checklist **Social validity** •IRP-15 (teacher) •CIRP (student) | The FABI will be faded once a functional relation is demonstrated using a validated single-case research design (e.g., withdrawal) and Behavior objective for the student is met (See BIP). |

Note. BASC-3 BESS = Behavior Assessment System for Children-Third Edition: Behavioral and Emotional Screening System (Kamphaus & Reynolds, 2015). IRP 15 = Intervention Rating Profile, CIRP = Child Intervention Rating Profile (Witt & Elliott, 1985). FABI Step Checklists are available from http://www.ci3t.org/fabi

# Implementation of an Initiative to LAUNCH: Supporting Systematic Change Efforts in One Early Childhood Community

*Melissa Stormont, Wendy Ell, Vicki Davolt, Rachel Kryah, Melody Boling, and Laine Young-Walker*

## Abstract

This article presents a community effort to build capacity for supporting early childhood social-emotional health across different early childhood contexts. Project LAUNCH, which was a grant supported effort, included a Wellness Council of key early childhood stakeholders who developed promotion and prevention goals for focusing efforts and data based systems for tracking progress. The results of the project across all targeted goals were promising and underscore the importance of community engagement in creating systemic change and establishing structures to promote and monitor specific practices in communities. Further, the prevention and promotion goals were supported across various contexts including early childhood physicians and professionals who conduct screening, families, and child care providers.

Keywords: Project LAUNCH, wellness, evidence-based, prevention, promotion

## Background

Young children with unidentified social-emotional concerns are at risk for continuing to experience problems when they enter elementary school. The window for primary prevention is in the early childhood period; if social, emotional, and mental health concerns are persistent, there is less that can be done to remediate them over time (Racz, King, Wu, Witkiewitz, & McMahon, 2013; Walker, 2004). Fortunately, research has identified the necessary components of comprehensive systems that prevent and address mental health challenges (Racz et al., 2013). The literature on mental health challenges indicates that communities can be successful in reducing challenging behavior when a proactive prevention and early intervention program is implemented (Stormont, Lewis, Beckner, & Johnson, 2008). The most effective early intervention approaches utilize several key components including screening, strengthening the skills of early child providers, parent aware-ness and education. The purpose of this article is to summarize a community effort to mobilize key partners and employ these evidence-based approaches to support mental health needs in young children and their parents. These efforts were possible due to grant funding to support the provision of personnel and resources needed to execute goals and achieve outcomes. The development of the project that was funded is described below.

## Development of Project LAUNCH Grant Proposal

Key stakeholders in the community were invited by a child psychiatrist (Division Chief of Child and Adolescent Psychiatry) at a Research One University for the discussion of submitting a Linking Actions for Unmet Needs in Children's Health (LAUNCH) grant. The Substance Abuse and Mental Health Services Administration (SAMHSA) federally funds LAUNCH grants. The purpose of Project LAUNCH is to promote wellness of young children from birth to age 8 by addressing the physical, social, emotional, cognitive, and behavioral aspects of their development. The reasons for involving the community partners in the discussion of the grant proposal and the development of the main activities were to a) secure buy in for the efforts and b) ensure the community stakeholders were, if funded, committed to working to support key jointly determined goals of the grant. Although these two are interrelated the latter is related to sustainability.

As a result, a group of early childhood stakeholders was brought together to discuss support of the SAMHSA Project LAUNCH Grant. There was discussion of the long-term goal of fostering the healthy development and wellness of all young children birth through age 8 in order to prepare them to thrive in school and beyond. If funded, the grant would improve coordination and collaboration across child-serving systems, improve access to higher quality care and evidence-based programs for young children and their families, and raise awareness and increase knowledge about young child wellness. The group was committed to continuing to work together regardless of grant funding. Therefore, securing commitment and buy-in during the grant proposal stage was a key defining feature for the partnerships that were formed within the context of the grant.

## County Demographics

The county where the grant was implemented is in central Missouri. At the time of implementation of LAUNCH there were 154,365 persons living in this county. The total population was 48.2% male and 51.8% female; 84.4% were Caucasian, 7.9% were African American, 0.4% were American Indian and Native, 3.1% were Asian, 0.1% were Native Hawaiian and Other Pacific Islander, 1.1% were some other race, 2.5% were Hispanic or Latino and 3.0% were two or more races; 10,000 were age 0–4 years of age and 9,055 were 5–9 years of age. The LAUNCH grant focused on children 0–8 years of age. At the time of the grant 19.1% of residents in this county lived in poverty whereas the state of Missouri had 14.6% of residents living in poverty (City-Data.com, n.d.) and 14.1% of households were enrolled in the food stamp program. During this time period, the number of children living in poverty and adult unemployment were increasing while programs to support children in poverty and subsidized childcare were decreasing and early child and mental health programs were also being cut to meet the state's budget deficit. The city data was used with the environmental scan the grant team conducted to determine increases and programs to serve children in poverty as well as those with mental health needs.

## Project LAUNCH

At the time the county received the grant, there were Project LAUNCH sites across the United States including: Arizona, Maine, New Mexico, Rhode Island, Washington, Red Cliff Band of Lake Superior Chippewa, California, District of Columbia, Iowa, Illinois, Kansas, Massachusetts, Michigan, New York, Ohio, Oregon, Wisconsin, Texas, Colorado, and Connecticut. The LAUNCH grant funded the work to improve coordination and collaboration, improve access to higher quality care and evidence-based programs, and raise awareness and increase knowledge about young child wellness, which were organized in core prevention strategies. The logic model is presented in Figure 1.

The grant award was for five years and a one-year no-cost extension was also provided. Key grant processes included the formation of a Wellness Council (WC), the ongoing utilization of this council, employment of an environmental scan, the creation of a mission, vision and core values of the group, development of a strategic plan, and implementation of prevention and promotion strategies.

### WC and Utilization of Council

After receiving the LAUNCH grant, a WC was formed. All early childhood stakeholders in the participating county were invited to join the council. The WC included representatives from a variety of organizations which served young children, including Head Start; pediatricians from two major practices; Parents as Teachers Organization; three county public schools systems; First Steps; First Chance for Children; Child Care Aware of Missouri; Parent Link; Rainbow House; Boone County Family Resources; United Way; County Health Department; Juvenile legal representation; Center for Family Policy and Research; the Missouri Department of Mental Health; Missouri Department of Health and Senior Services, Section for Healthy Families and Youth; Center for Autism and Neurodevelopmental Disorders.

The WC met monthly. Initial meetings were focused on getting to know the other members of the council. Time was spent introducing each organization and what it had to offer young children. As a group the Council also discussed hopes and dreams for early child interventions in Boone County. After these introductory meetings, the Council focused on creating a mission, vision, and values for the group. The WC continuously monitored the project goals and served to support and encourage all partners.

## Environmental Scan

An environmental scan was conducted by searching online for mental health services available within the community. The purpose of the environmental scan was to determine community-based, evidence-based services for young children with mental health concerns and their families. The searches yielded numerous agencies that were then evaluated based upon whether the agencies listed evidence-based practices in their information. Follow up contacts were also made to verify results or to solicit information regarding the use of evidence-based practices when the information was not easily located online. At the time of the scan, no evidence-based therapy services were known to be available for children age 0–3 years old or their parents. The environmental scan helped to guide the WC in the creation of a strategic plan and initiatives to address core prevention and promotion strategies.

## Strategic Plan: Mission and Vision

Our shared mission was to develop an accessible, seamless early childhood system for all children, age 0–8, and families in Boone County. By harnessing resources and coordinating and integrating evidence-based practices focused on awareness and prevention, we aimed to support a continuum of services that would empower all adults to be responsible for young children's health and development. Our vision statement was "a nurturing community that enhances the health and wellness of children and families, allowing them to reach their full potential." The core prevention and promotion strategies were screening and assessment, family strengthening and parent skills training, and mental health consultation in early care and education.

## Implementation of Core Strategies

As we focused on each of the following core prevention and promotion strategies we identified the elements which already existed in the county and attempted to leverage them before creating something new. The efforts around this work in the community included ensuring the following core strategies: ongoing collection of data on needs, evaluating barriers for implementation, understanding any aspect of the grant activities that were not effective in their practical implementation, and assessing consumer satisfaction for interventions. The research literature is clear on the need for this type of data to ensure evidence-based practices can actually be implemented well within real world settings (Fixsen, Naoom, Blasé, Friedman, & Wallace, 2005). As such, the WC monitored the grant activities utilizing the logic model (see Figure 1). Participants within each core strategy are discussed in the following sections.

### Screening in a Variety of Child Serving Settings

The WC established a workgroup to devise a plan to meet the prevention goal of universal screening in a variety of child serving settings. Ten people reflective of the early childhood community in the county (including pediatricians, home visitors, mental health professionals, and Parents as Teachers Organization) were included in the workgroup. A main goal of this group was to identify a screening tool that was evidence-based, which was also a requirement of the LAUNCH grant. A few agencies were utilizing the Ages and Stages Questionnaire-Second Edition (ASQ-2) and the Ages and Stages Questionnaire Social-emotional (ASQ-SE), for developmental screening. The ASQ-Third Edition (ASQ-3) had recently been published. The work group chose to use the ASQ-3 and the ASQ-SE because of their strong psychometric properties, engagement of parents and ease of use. Training was provided to the community agencies in the WC through a train-the-trainer model. The LAUNCH grant supported agencies with the provision of ASQ screening kits, and paid for the training, thus providing needed infrastructure to support the adoption of screening.

Goals identified for the training included increasing universal, evidence-based developmental screening and, in particular, social-emotional screening. At the time, many providers and agencies were only using informal observation to screen development and not screening for social-emotional health. One of the barriers which prevented screening was the lack of knowledge regarding where to refer children if they tested positive on the screening. Members of the WC identified this referral barrier and the need to create a list of referral options for families when children needed more assessment or intervention. A referral matrix was created as a remedy.

Overall, prior to this intervention there were fragmented efforts without a consistent evidence-based screening tool. The WC identified the ASQ-3 and the ASQ-SE as the tools to use consistently in the community, trained the community to provide the screenings, and provided them with a referral matrix to use when children were identified.

## Parenting Interventions

The Incredible Years BASIC Parenting Program (IY) and parent cafés were used as the methods of enhancing parenting skills and providing training. Briefly, the IY is a series of evidence-based programs for parents, children, and teachers. The goals of IY are to strengthen parent competencies and involvement in children's school experiences to promote academic, social and emotional development and reduce conduct problems (Webster-Stratton, 2015). The IY framework has been successful in promoting social, emotional, and academic competence and reducing young children's behavior problems. It has been shown to be applicable to all cultures and socioeconomic groups.

There were several persons in the community who had IY parent training and felt it was a great program that could be utilized to enhance the skills of parents in this county. The LAUNCH grant supported the training of five additional persons to deliver IY in the county. In order to support implementation of the IY model, an organized learning community of providers trained in IY met bi-monthly. Those trained through LAUNCH and those already implementing IY were invited to attend. Parents were recruited from urban and rural areas of the county to participate in IY parenting groups. This allowed IY groups to occur in the largest city in the county and in rural areas as well. Prior to IY Parenting groups, there were limited options for parents to access group interventions which would support and enhance parenting skills. Boone County LAUNCH conducted eight IY parenting groups.

After successful implementation of IY, Boone County LAUNCH directed efforts to conduct parent cafés. A second LAUNCH program (Missouri LAUNCH) had been very successful in bringing parent cafes to the St. Louis, Missouri area. Implementation in Boone County occurred through a partnership with Missouri LAUNCH. The parent cafes provided an opportunity for parents to come together to build a support network around the Center for Studies in Social Policy's evidence-based strengthening families' protective factors. These factors focused on parental resilience, social connections, concrete support, knowledge of parenting and child development, and social-emotional competence of children. The cafes' goals included creating a community/social skill network around parenting issues and enhancing the parenting skills of those who participate. This LAUNCH grant partnered with Missouri LAUNCH to train providers to implement parent cafés in the county. The goals for this part of the project were to train parents and community agency teams to implement parent cafés in the community and to secure agreement from them that they would implement the cafés in the community. Evaluation of the parent cafés focused on the ability to deliver the training to a cohort of parents and agency teams in the community who were willing to lead this effort.

## Prevention in Early Childhood Centers

Although teachers can implement early social-behavioral supports, such practices are not common across multiple systems in one program, district or state (Stormont et al., 2008). Ensuring children receive appropriate support for their developmental needs in the early childhood years is challenging due to the lack of standardization across multiple systems, with different requirements for early childcare and preschool programs (e.g., education level, certification, knowledge of development and developmentally appropriate practices; Brawley & Stormont, 2014; Kim, Stormont, & Espinosa, 2009). Thus, the WC and LAUNCH workgroup selected improving teachers' knowledge of social behavioral supports as a target goal for the grant.

Early Childhood-Positive Behavioral Interventions and Support (EC-PBIS), as applied in this county, is a model of Early Childhood Mental Health Consultation (ECMHC), which combines the framework, principles, and resources of two evidence-based programs: Pyramid Model for Supporting Social-emotional Competence in Infant/Toddlers and Young Children (CSEFEL) and Positive Behavior Interventions and Supports (PBIS or PBS). Several school districts in the county utilized PBS, and utilization of EC-PBS in pre-schools would enhance school readiness by making transition to a kindergarten that implemented PBS smoother for children. EC-PBS is a system of ongoing training and support in the area of social-emotional-behavioral functioning for early childhood professionals in their programs. Programmatic services include training for EC-PBS, on-site coaching of programs, teams and classrooms, and technical assistance and instructional resources for early childhood professionals.

Within the integrated model implemented in this project, a coaching aspect was employed to provide support to teachers as they were implementing new skills in their classrooms. Coaching is essential, as it is challenging for teachers to integrate new teaching practices into applied settings. Research on traditional professional development has documented numerous times that teachers do not transfer skills related to implementation of social-emotional supports for children from professional inservice training to their classrooms (e.g., Stormont, Smith, & Lewis, 2006).

The main training goals were to enhance childcare providers' knowledge and skills, improve the classrooms in childcare settings, strengthen the relationships between childcare providers and children/parents, and prepare young children for kindergarten. Eleven early childhood sites, six clustered in three rural towns, participated in the program. The participants included 80 early childhood professionals and 400 children located in centers, preschools, and home-based care. After the training, six EC-PBS coaches worked to support implementation of the positive behavior support strategies in practice settings. The coaches all held bachelor's or master's degrees in social work, human development, or education. All coaches were trained on ASQ-3 and ASQ-SE screenings and EC-PBS by the lead mental health consultant. Coaches were also supervised. During their coaching sessions with teachers, coaches worked to provide teachers with strategies to build positive relationships with children, families, peers, create environments that support positive behavior, implement social emotional strategies and practices, and recognize the need for individualized intervention.

## Measures

Across each of the grant prevention and promotion goals, measures were used to evaluate progress toward each of the goals. These are described below.

## Parental Stress Scale

The Parental Stress Scale (PSS) is a measure of stress associated with parenting and includes 18 items, which are rated on a 5-point scale (1 = strongly disagree and 5 = strongly agree). For this project, the PSS was administered at the beginning of the program and again upon program completion. The PSS has strong psychometric properties and is frequently used as a measure of stress as a dependent variable (Nam, Wikoff, & Sherraden, 2015; Tervo, 2012).

## Parenting Scale

The Incredible Years Parenting Scale (IYPS) is a measure designed to assess parenting skills. Each item is rated on a seven-point scale with low scores representing effective parenting and high scores representing ineffective parenting. The scale is comprised of three subscales: 1) laxness (11 items), 2) overreactivity (10 items) and 3) verbosity (7 items). To evaluate program outcomes, participants completed the IYPS at the beginning of the program and again upon program completion.

## PreSET

The Preschool-wide Evaluation Tool (Pre-SET) was developed to accurately assess and evaluate the implementation status of primary-universal program-wide positive behavior support in early childhood settings (Horner, Benedict, & Todd, 2005). All items included on the Pre-SET were informed by current research on program-wide positive behavior support (PW-PBS) in early childhood settings and developmentally appropriate practice. The Pre-SET assesses classroom and program-wide variables across eight categories related to primary universal features of PW-PBS: expectations defined, behavioral expectations taught, responses to appropriate and challenging behavior, organized and predictable environment, monitoring and decision-making, family involvement, and management and program support (Horner et al., 2005). The lead early childhood mental health consultant used the Pre-SET to assess the implementation of the EC-PBS program.

## Results and Discussion

### Prevention and Promotion Goal 1: Screening

This project was successful in training the workforce to provide developmental screenings. Specifically, 519 providers were trained to deliver the ASQ-3 and the ASQ-SE screenings. Participants reported an increase in their knowledge and attitudes around developmental screening and referral activities from pretest to posttest. Increases in screening were seen in a large pediatric practice and in the community. The pediatric practice had a physician champion who helped move the effort forward. Prior to the ASQ training one large pediatric office was not screening. After training and support, this practice completed 4,036 ASQ-3 screenings and 220 ASQ-SE screenings (Young-Walker, Stormont, Buecke, & Ell, 2017).

Community screening outreach efforts included 54 screening events at the local library, Women Infants and Children (WIC), parent groups, and at the Child Welfare Office (i.e., foster care). Screenings and referrals peaked in the final years of the grant. These increases were primarily due to the support the ASQ consultation provided to trained early childhood professionals, particularly in the EC-PBS program, to the installment of Patient Tools (PTI) and to the implementation of the Healthy Steps for Young Children in one of the largest pediatric clinics in Boone County. In the no-cost year, six of the grant providers were trained in the updated ASQ:SE-2. The total number of screenings, in the county, over the life of the grant included 11,688 children screened with the ASQ-3 and 2793 with the ASQ:SE or ASQ:SE-2. Also, 872 referrals were made using the ASQ-3 and 118 using the ASQ:SE or ASQ:SE-2. See Figure 2 for screening data by group.

The findings suggest Boone County LAUNCH was very successful at increasing developmental screening and referral efforts throughout the county. It is evident that having a champion pediatrician increased Boone County LAUNCH's ability to implement screening in the pediatrician setting and that early childcare professionals are highly successful in the implementation of screening when given support and consultation. Through these efforts, it was evident that screening in community settings is a reliable and effective way to reach parents and screen children that might not otherwise be reached. There is a clear need to prioritize screenings for children at higher risk of developmental and behavioral concerns, particularly children in foster care.

These results demonstrate the need for an increase in developmental screenings by trained providers (e.g., physician, home visitors, and childcare workers), particularly when training is paired with consultation. Another critical piece to success was providing trained providers with a current referral matrix and community resource list to use when screening results indicated children were at risk in specific developmental domains.

## Prevention Goal 2: Increase Parenting Skills

**Incredible Years.** To examine the impact of the IY Basic Parenting Program on the Parental Stress Scale, a paired-samples t-test was conducted. There was a statistically significant decrease in scores from pre ($M = 37.51$, $SD = 9.05$) to post ($M = 33.94$, $SD = 8.97$), $t$ (53) = 3.97 $p$ <.001 (two-tailed). The mean decrease in scores on the Parental Stress Scale was 3.57 with a 95% confidence interval ranging from 1.76 to 5.37. The Cohen's $d$ statistic (.37) indicated a small effect size. The significant decrease in scores on the Parental Stress Scale suggests that completion of the IY Basic Parenting Program was associated with reductions in stress associated with parenting.

A paired-samples t-test was conducted to evaluate the impact of the IY BASIC Parenting Program on the IYPS. Overall, there was statistically significant decrease in scores from pre ($M = 3.40$, $SD$ =.65) to post ($M = 2.60$, $SD = .59$), $t$ (49) = 9.11, $p$ <.001 (two-tailed).

The mean decrease in IYPS scores was .80 with a 95% confidence interval ranging from .62 to .97. The Cohen's *d* statistic (1.29) indicated a large effect size. In addition to the overall score, each of the three (3) subscales was also examined. Statistically significant decreases were observed for scores on each of the subscales. The significant decrease in overall scores, as well as scores on each subscale, suggests that completion of the IY BASIC Parenting Program was associated with the use of more effective parenting skills.

**Parent café trainings:** Training parents to run brief parent groups. Project LAUNCH hosted a two-day parent café training in Columbia, Missouri. A total of 34 participants attended the trainings and approximately half of those attending were associated with Boone County Project Launch. Teams of parents and professionals attended the trainings. Most of the participants were female (day 1:71% and day 2:67%) and were attending the training as professionals (62.5% and 71.4%). On both days, over half (59% and 53%) of the participants reported their race/ethnicity as Caucasian and over a third were African American (41% and 47%). Participants reported being from a number of agencies including Parent Link (41.2% and 33.3%), Boys and Girls Club (29% and 33%) and a city housing authority (29% and 33%). Post-test findings indicate satisfaction with the training, with around 70% of participants rating it as "great" overall. Ratings of the facilitators and handouts/materials were also high. However, the timing, pace, and organization were rated slightly lower. After the second day of training, 100% agreed that they were ready to host a parent café. Additionally, after the second day of training almost half (47%) of participants were "very much" looking forward to hosting parent cafés. These findings suggest that the trainings were effective at preparing and motivating the trainees for the parent café.

Participants indicated they liked a number of aspects of the trainings. Many responded they liked the group interaction and learning from others. Several participants noted they liked having the opportunity to practice implementing the parent café.

Participants thought the trainers were enthusiastic and engaging and felt the training increased their knowledge and awareness of the information presented. When asked to list three principles, points, or ideas from the trainings that stood out, participant responses included communication, taking time to listen, building positive relationships, protective factors, respect, importance of confidentiality, making agreements instead of rules, and being supportive and understanding instead of judgmental. The most common responses from participants when asked three actions they would take as a result of the trainings were planning and hosting a parent café. Other participants chose taking care of themselves, training others, listening, focusing on protective factors, communicating effectively, and overall applying the skills they have learned from the trainings at home.

## Prevention Goal 3: Increase Childcare Worker Knowledge and Skills

Two sources of data were used to explore the impact grant activities around training and supporting early childhood PBS had on promoting early childhood mental health; data were collected using the PreSET (implementation fidelity) and on screening for children in childcare settings (reported above).

The PreSET results were positive; two (2) of the seven (7) sites reached full implementation and five (5) additional sites are within 8 percentage points of reaching the 80% implementation goal. In addition to overall PreSET scores, the PreSET assesses classroom and program-wide variables across eight categories related to primary universal features of program-wide positive behavior support (PW-PBS). At follow up, the percentage of PreSET features implemented range from 67% to 90% (see Figure 3). The categories within the PreSET were used to guide needs for coaching. For example, category A (expectations defined; ⇩8%) and category H (program support; ⇩10%) decreased over the course of the grant and were areas for coaching. According to the early-childhood professional coaches, the main reason why there was a decrease in the "expectations defined" category was due to sites not incorporating a matrix of classroom rules and routines in their classroom. Ongoing coaching and support is clearly needed to support site implementation of PW-PBS.

## Conclusions

The need to increase community capacity to support the social, emotional, and mental health of young children is clear. Many children have significant mental health needs and need early intervention. Furthermore, parents and early childcare providers also need to be able to provide support for social-emotional development. Therefore, it is critical that agencies and professionals who focus on early childhood and work with families and children of young children have access to training and support in best practices in screening and interventions. Further, early childhood educators are on the front line in working to support the development of young children; it is important they have appropriate screening and support strategies to promote the social-emotional development of young children. This project reflects a wide-scale community effort to employ a nuanced, yet focused set of activities and strategies to meet main project goals. Lessons learned include the importance of training community members in selected evidence-based strategies, employing screening linked with referral options, and having individuals committed to advancing the goals of the project through championing efforts and helping overcome any barriers to implementation.

### References

Berry, J. D., & Jones, W.H. (1995). The Parental Stress Scale: Initial psychometric evidence. *Journal of Social and Personal Relationships, 12,* 463–472.

Brawley, S., & Stormont, M. (2014). Investigating reported data practices in early childhood: An exploratory study. *Journal of Positive Behavior Interventions, 16,* 102–111.

City-Data.com (n.d.) Retrieved from http://www.city-data.com/

Horner, R.H., Benedict, E.A., & Todd, A. (2005). *Preschool-wide evaluation tool.* Eugene, OR: Educational and Community Supports.

Kim, Y. H., Stormont, M., & Espinosa, L. (2009). Contributing factors to South Korean early childhood educators' strategies for addressing children's challenging behavior. *Journal of Early Intervention, 31,* 227–249.

Nam, Y., Wikoff, N., & Sherraden, M. (2015). Racial and ethnic differences in parenting stress: Evidence from a statewide sample of new mothers. *Journal of Child and Family Studies, 24*(2), 278–288. doi:10.1007/s10826-013-9833-z

Racz, S.J., King, K.M., Wu, J., Witkiewitz, K., & McMahon, R.J. (2013). The predictive utility of a brief kindergarten screening measure of child behavior problems. *Journal of Consulting and Clinical Psychology, 81,* 588–599.

Stormont, M., Lewis, T. J., Beckner, R., & Johnson, N. W. (2008). *Implementing systems of positive behavior support systems in early childhood and elementary settings.* Thousand Oaks, CA: Corwin Press.

Stormont, M., Covington, S., & Lewis, T. J. (2006). Using data to inform systems: Assessing teacher implementation of key features of positive behavior support. *Beyond Behavior, 15*(3), 10–14.

Tervo, R. (2012). Developmental and behavior problems predict parenting stress in young children with global delay. *Journal of Child Neurology, 27,* 291–296.

Walker, H. M. (2004). Commentary: Use of evidence-based intervention in schools: Where we've been, where we are, and where we need to go. *School Psychology Review, 33*(3), 398–407.

Webster-Stratton, C. (2015). The Incredible Years Series: A review of the independent research base. *Journal of Child and Family Studies, 24,* 1898–1916.

Young-Walker, L., Stormont, M., Buecke, N., & Ell, W. (2017). Supporting increased screening in the pediatric population. *Perspectives on Early Childhood Psychology and Education, 2,* 115–128.

**Figure 1.**
*Project Logic Model*

| Project Launch Logic Model *Increasing Early Childhood Wellness Through Community Collaboration and Increased Education, Training, and Awareness* | | |
|---|---|---|
| **Resources (inputs)** | **Program prevention and promotion** | **Activities** |
| People: •Staff including, psychiatrists, •Wellness council  Data: •Environmental scan  Funds: •Grant funds •Operating budget •Partner funds | 1. Create a coordinated system to improve screening in a variety of settings | 1a. Created a local council on child wellness including multiple early child stakeholders 1b. Strengthen the infrastructure necessary to support, expand, and sustain capacity to provide a screening (trained providers in train the trainer model for ASQ 1c. Created referral matrix |
| | 2. Family strengthening and parent skills training. | 2a. Trained providers in IY 2b. Provided IY to parents 2c. Provided parent café's |
| | 3. Early child care provider (teachers) strengthening including ways to enhance screening and supports for social and emotional development in young children. | 3a. Trained childcare providers on social-emotional development of young children and needs for positive behavior supports (EC-PBS) 3b. Trained childcare providers to use the ASQ and ASQ-SE 3c. Provided weekly onsite coaching |

**Figure 1.**
*Project Logic Model (continued)*

| Project Launch Logic Model<br>*Increasing Early Childhood Wellness Through Community Collaboration and Increased Education, Training, and Awareness* | |
| --- | --- |
| **Intermediate outcomes** | **Evaluation data** |
| 1a. Increased capacity in the child-serving system through collaboration and coordination.<br>1b. Improved access to evidence-based screening | 1a. Increased number of providers trained in use of evidence-based screening<br>1b. Increased screening with evidence-based tool<br>1c. Increased referrals for developmental needs |
| 2a. Increased parental knowledge of problem behaviors and emotions<br>2c. Increased protective factors and decreased risk factors in children age 0–8 | 2a. Increased parental resilience<br>2b. Decreased parental stress<br>2c. Increase number of parents trained to support other parents in community |
| 3a. Increased provider and community knowledge of the importance of early childhood mental health services<br>3b. Increased ability to detect children with developmental delays due to screening<br>3c. Improved classrooms behavioral interventions from regular coaching | 3a. Increased use of EC-PBS features at child care centers<br>3b. Increase screening in child-care settings |

**Figure 2.**
*ASQ-3 and ASQ-SE Community Screenings*

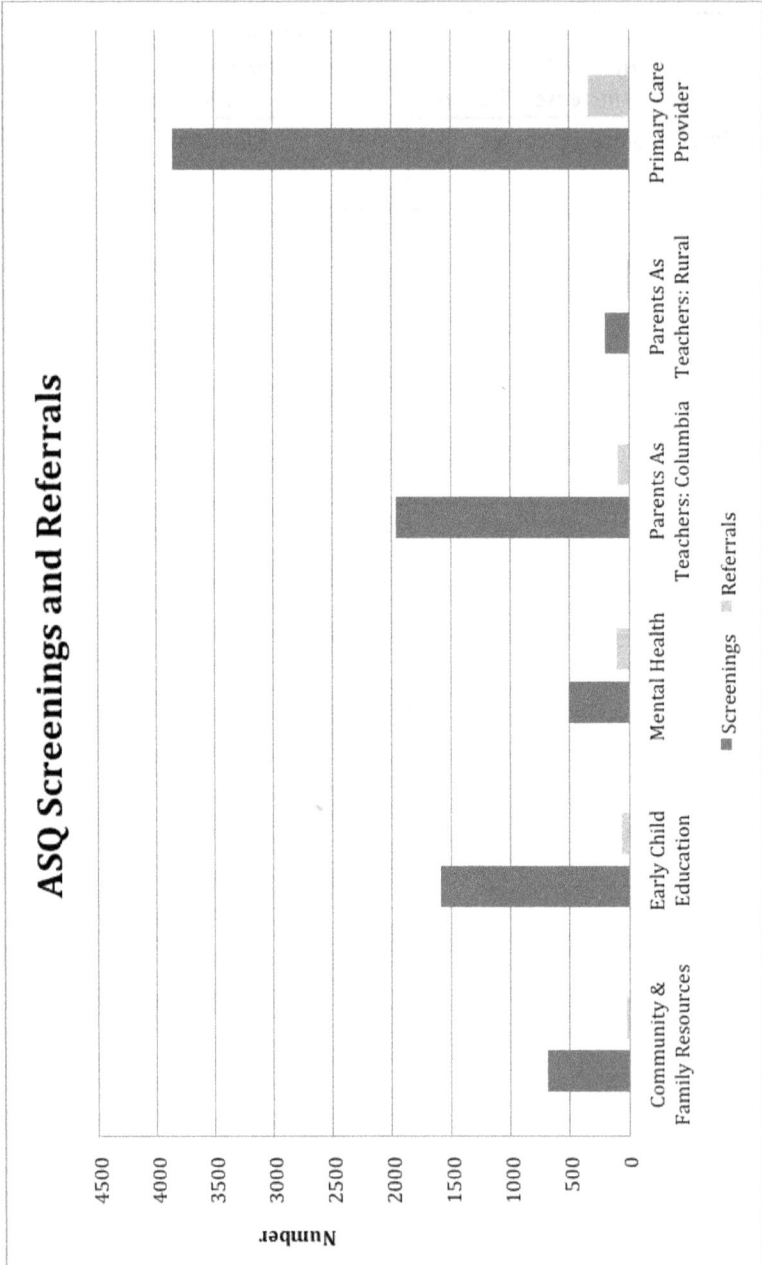

**Figure 3.**
*PreSet category scores at before and after EC-PBS training*

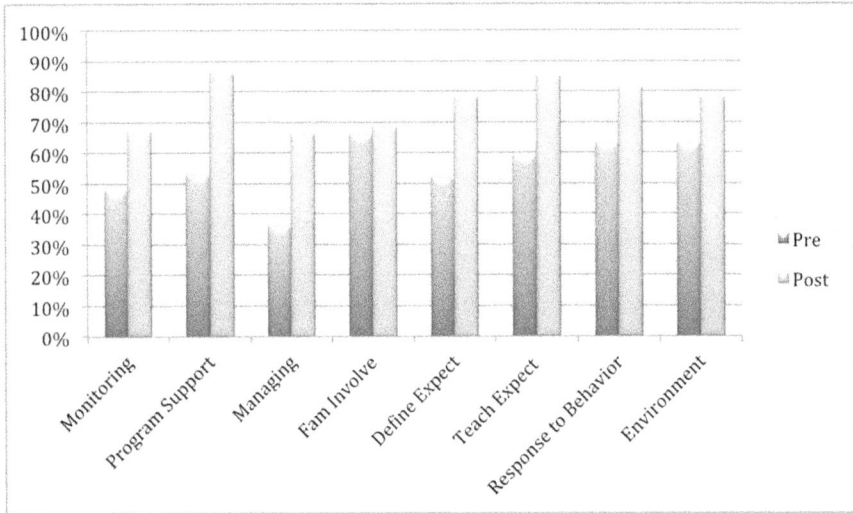

**Figure 4.**
*Demographics of ASQ-3 Training Participants (N = 246)*

| Item | N | % of participants |
|---|---|---|
| **Gender** | | |
| Female | 217 | 96% |
| **Age** | | |
| Average | 217 | 34 |
| Range | | 18–82 |
| **Race** | | |
| Caucasian | 106 | 84% |
| African American | 14 | 10% |
| **Employee type** | | |
| Medical doctor | 2 | 1% |
| Other medical care provider | 10 | 5% |
| Child care provider | 114 | 52% |
| Teacher | 37 | 17% |
| Social worker | 9 | 4% |
| Director/administrator | 3 | 1% |
| Other | 44 | 20% |
| **Education** | | |
| High school graduate or higher | 125 | 98% |

*Note. ASQ-3 = Ages and Stages Questionnaire-Third Edition*

*Figure 4.* Demographics of ASQ-SE Training Participants (*N* = 75).

| Item | *N* | % of participants |
|---|---|---|
| **Gender** | | |
| **Female** | 72 | 96% |
| Age | | |
| Average | 75 | 34 |
| Range | | 17–61 |
| **Race** | | |
| Caucasian | 56 | 74% |
| African American | 16 | 21% |
| **Employee Type** | | |
| Child care provider | 33 | 43% |
| Teacher | 30 | 39% |
| Social worker | 4 | 5% |
| School administrator | 1 | 1% |
| Other | 8 | 11% |
| **Education** | | |
| High school graduate or higher | 70 | 91% |

*Note. ASQ-SE = Ages and Stages Questionnaire Social-Emotional*

# Prevention of Behavior Problems through Increasing Culturally Responsive Pedagogy in Early Childhood Settings

*Ambra L. Green, Jennifer M. McKenzie,*
*and Melissa Stormont*

## Abstract

Children of color and children from diverse backgrounds are more likely to experience exclusionary discipline practice, as amply demonstrated by recent data. This is a moral and ethical concern for the field of education and early childhood education in particular. The data validate the research that continues to advocate the need for practitioners to use evidence-based and culturally responsive instructional, behavioral, and family engagement practices. The purpose of this article is to discuss how evidence-based and culturally responsive practices for early childhood educators can close disparities found among children of color, especially children of color at-risk for mental health and behavioral concerns, and prevent inaccurate referrals to special education for behavioral disorders.

Keywords: prevention, behavior, mental health, early childhood, disparities, culturally responsive pedagogy

The start of formal education in early childhood programs is a critical period in the lives of young children. For some young children, preschool or kindergarten marks the beginning of several years of experience learning new concepts, skills, and vocabulary in environments that hold values and ideologies corresponding to those found in their own homes (Barnett, Carolan, & Johns, 2013). The majority of these same young children are likely to continue to benefit from these types of educational environments through graduation. For others though, the early childhood era marks the beginning of disparities and differential treatment in education (and related areas) to be experienced for years to come (Barnett et al., 2013). The vast differences between the early childhood experiences of many white children and children of color, particularly African American children, have been consistent over time and are arguably the foundation of the preschool-to-prison pipeline (Adamu & Hogan, 2015).

The preschool-to-prison pipeline can be defined as the policies, procedures, and practices, whether overt or covert, that push students out of school and toward the criminal justice system. One example of such a practice is that students of color are disproportionally excluded from the learning environment for minor classroom behaviors (Skiba, Albrecht, & Losen, 2013). For example, African American preschool students lead their peers of all races in rates of out-of-school suspension (OSS; U.S. Department of Education, 2016). Such disparities continue into K–12 schools. According to the Civil Rights Data Collection Survey, African American students in K–12 schools are 3.8 times more likely to receive one or more OSS compared to their white peers (U.S. Department of Education Office of Civil Rights, 2014). These disparities continue for African American students with disabilities in K–12 settings. African American students with disabilities are 2.8 times more likely than other students to receive suspension or expulsion. Whereas African American students with disabilities represent about 19% of the population of students with disabilities, they comprise about 46% of students receiving OSS (U.S. Department of Education, 2016) and are more likely to be referred to special education for behavioral reasons (Skiba et al., 2013).

There are many areas in which early childhood programs can aid in the prevention of unnecessary referrals for special education services, exclusionary discipline practices, and the preschool-to-prison pipeline for young children of color. The purpose of this article is two-fold. First, the article focuses on three contributors in early childhood to the onset of the preschool-to-prison pipeline. The second purpose is to discuss how evidence-based and culturally responsive practices for early childhood educators should be utilized while seeking to close disparities found among children of color, especially children of color at risk for mental health and behavioral concerns, and prevent inaccurate referrals to special education for behavioral disorders.

## At the Onset of the Pipeline

The lack of early identification of supportive services for students of color who may be at risk for mental health issues likely contribute to the preschool-to-prison pipeline. Mental health services, discipline disparities, and opportunity gaps are discussed as early contributors to the pipeline. By highlighting contributors, educators can identify areas in which prevention can serve as a change agent.

### Mental Health Services

Mental health is a key component of student success, beginning at birth and continuing through the formative years of early childhood education. Unfortunately, students whose earliest experiences create "toxic stress"—levels of stress that are so high and consistent that children cannot learn and develop at normal rates (Knitzer & Lefkowitz, 2006)—are especially susceptible to social and emotional difficulties. Various demographic, child, family, and environmental factors have been shown to cause toxic stress and increase the risk of developing mental health issues. Being raised by a single or unemployed parent, receiving public assistance, and having a parent who lacks a high school diploma or general education diploma (GED) have been associated with increased levels of risk (Shonkoff et al., 2004). Additionally, more significant parental risk factors associated with poor developmental and emotional outcomes for children include maternal depression (Hay, Pawlby, Angold, Harold, & Sharp, 2003), domestic violence (Appleyard, Egeland, Dulmen, & Sroufe, 2005; Edleson, 1999), and stressful family circumstances, such as family conflict and mental illness in the family (Coie et al., 1993).

The current mental health service delivery model is inadequate to meet the needs of young children and their families, especially those from diverse racial and ethnic groups, who are less likely to receive services than white children (Pires, Grimes, Allen, Gilmer, & Mahadevan, 2013). Only 13% of children of color receive mental health services, compared to 31% of white children (Pires et al., 2013). Among children in the child welfare system, African American children have less access to counseling than white children (Wells, Hillemeier, Bai, & Belue, 2009). Culture, or more specifically, cultural mismatch, can also be a risk factor in the development of mental health issues and/or behavioral problems. The cultural mismatch hypothesis holds that teachers or service providers are more likely to inappropriately refer, identify, make placements for, and discipline students of color because they do not understand or are dismissive of their cultures (Skiba et al., 2008). Culture influences human development, including how adults view childhood mental health, expectations for young children, and child rearing practices of parents and caregivers (McMiller & Weisz, 1996). The lack of an effective service delivery model has significant implications for the discipline and provision of appropriate interventions and identification of young children with and at-risk for mental health disorders served within early childhood programs.

## Discipline Disparities of Students with Mental Health Disorders

Despite the presence of characteristics of an emotional-behavioral disorder (EBD) in young children, identification is often delayed until further in the elementary level (Kauffman & Landrum, 2013). Research suggests that approximately 10% to 20% of young children engage in behaviors that place them at-risk for an EBD (Dunlap et al., 2006) and, because these children have not been identified, they receive instruction in classrooms with teachers who believe they are unprepared to best serve the needs of these children (Niesyn, 2009). The need for educator competency regarding how best to serve students with mental health concerns, as well as cultural influences that may affect teachers' view of behavior, is crucial. The inaccurate referrals and identification of young children of color with disabilities is detrimental, as it maintains educational and access disparities between children of color and their white peers.

The literature is replete with data illustrating inaccurate referrals for special education services, specifically for mental health related disorders (Skiba et al., 2013; Sullivan, Van Norman, & Klingbeil, 2014), and exclusionary discipline practices received by students of color with disabilities (U.S. Department of Education, 2016). While these data have been reported for over 40 years (Donovan & Cross, 2002; Dunn, 1968; Heller, Holtzman, & Messick, 1982; Oswald, Coutinho, Best, & Singh, 1999), the extent to which young children of color receive exclusionary discipline practices has only recently been reported (U.S. Department of Education, 2016). The most recent Civil Rights Data Collection Survey reports that while African American children represent 19% of the preschool population, they represent 47% of children receiving one or more OSS (U.S. Department of Education Office of Civil Rights, 2014). When compared to their white preschool peers, African American preschool children are 3.6 times as likely to receive one or more OSS. Such high rates of suspension and expulsion lead to many hours of lost instruction per year (Scott & Barrett, 2004) which further exacerbates the academic disparities between students of color and their white peers.

## Opportunity Gap

Research has clearly documented that when comparing the academic achievement of students of color and white students, students of color consistently perform at lower rates (Vanneman, Hamilton, Baldwin, Anderson, & Rahman, 2009). Analysis into reasons why this might be revealed an opportunity gap, in which students of color are more likely to be educated in under-resourced educational settings, taught by underprepared or less-experienced teachers, and have a lack of access to quality instruction and opportunities

(Barnett et al., 2013). In particular, African American children and children from low socioeconomic status homes lack access to high-quality early education (Barnett et al., 2013).

The White House Initiative of Educational Excellence for African-Americans (WHIEAA) and the National Institute for Early Education Research used National Center for Education Statistics data to measure the quality of early care and education for African American students. Utilizing the Early Childhood Environment Rating Scale (ECERS) to measure community-based settings and the Family Day Care Rating Scale (FDCRS) to measure home-based settings, findings indicate that about 15% of African American children attended child care centers ranked "low"; almost double the percentage of Latino and white children (Barnett et al., 2013). Further, the majority of Head Start programs, the largest federal prevention effort aimed to prepare children in low-income communities for kindergarten were found to be of "medium" quality (Barnett et al., 2013). Additionally, while the likelihood that white or Latino children attended "high-quality" Head Start programs is about 50%, the likelihood that African American children attended "high-quality" programs was only about 26%. This lack of access to quality programs can lead to a deficit in readiness that results in unprepared young children entering elementary schools. Barnett and colleagues (2013) report that if the educational needs of young children are inadequately met in the first five years of life, they are likely to fall behind their peers before they even begin kindergarten.

The disparities experienced by children of color, especially African American children, exist within multiple sectors and related areas of education. Some of these disparities are found at the beginning of the preschool-to-prison pipeline, while others maintain the process. To prevent gaps in achievement and opportunity, inaccurate referrals for special education services (Skiba et al., 2013), and reduce the overrepresentation of young children of color receiving exclusionary discipline practices (U.S. Department of Education, 2016), early childhood educators must be consistent in their implementation of evidence-based practices (EBP) and culturally relevant pedagogy (CRP; Green & Stormont, 2017) while increasing efforts to engage families.

## Culturally Relevant Pedagogy: What We Teach

Cholewa, Goodman, West-Olatunji, and Amatea (2014) assert that education in the nation's schools "consists of more than just reading, writing, and mathematics; it advances a specific Eurocentric worldview" (p. 578). This Eurocentric worldview—defined as a focus on European cultural practices, expectations, and behaviors while regarding European culture as preeminent—can be seen in the misinterpretation of behavior and misidentification of ability for children of color. Historically, however, attempts to mitigate educational disparities, specifically in academic achievement, have not acknowledged this bias. Rather, they have utilized deficit-focused frameworks; frameworks that conceptualize underperformance as a result of a child's and their family's personal or cultural limitations (Walker, 2011).

A more recent body of literature has emerged assessing the relationships between systemic oppression, cultural mismatch, and educational hegemony and the potential for associated emotional and psychological effects (Brody et al., 2006; Goodman & West-Olatunji, 2010). Educational hegemony relates to the dominance of Eurocentric values and ideologies as the traditional educational practices within schools (Goodman & West-Olatunji, 2010). Goodman and West-Olatunji (2010) found that students of color may have experiences within the classroom that increase their levels of stress and perceptions of discrimination, since educational settings tend to reinforce the broader context of hegemony. Further, the stress caused by children having to navigate between school and home cultures has been associated with increased depression and decreased self-esteem for students of color (Brody et al., 2006; Romero, Martinez, & Carvajal, 2007), each of which are characteristic of mental health issues. This body of research, along with

Bronfenbrenner's (1994) ecological-framework, supports the need for pedagogy that bridges the dissonance between Eurocentric views in schools and the cultures of the students they serve.

Culturally-relevant pedagogy (CRP), with an emphasis on teaching diverse populations of students through their own racial and ethnic identities, cultural experiences, and perspectives (Gay, 2013) has been proven as one mechanism for addressing such dissonance. CRP is defined by Ladson-Billings (1995) as:

> A pedagogy of oppression not unlike critical pedagogy but specifically committed to collective, not merely individually, empowerment. Culturally relevant pedagogy rests on three criteria or propositions: (a) students must experience academic success; (b) students must develop and/or maintain cultural competence; and (c) students must develop a critical consciousness through which they challenge the status quo of the current social order (p. 160)

Current research on the achievement of African American students mostly focuses on the use of culturally-relevant pedagogy and practices (Irvine, 2012; Townsend, 2000). Qualitative research has identified CRP as a way for schools to acknowledge the home and community cultures of their students while sensitively integrating their cultural experiences, values, and understandings into the learning environment (Brown-Jeffy & Cooper, 2011). The academic achievement of culturally diverse learners will improve when taught through cultural filters (Townsend, 2000).

## Experiencing Academic Success

Significant focus has been paid to students in K–12 educational settings, yet the differences in knowledge and skills between children of color and white children have been shown to appear before age three (Barnett et al., 2013). CRP helps educators of young children provide opportunities for students of color to feel successful academically. Because young children enter early childhood programs with a wide variety of previous educational experiences, educators must think strategically about how to provide these opportunities and develop lesson plans accordingly (Green & Stormont, 2017). The use of EBPs such as assessing task difficulty (Treptow, Burns, & McComas, 2007; Umbreit, Lane, & Dejud, 2004), providing increased opportunities to respond (Lambert, Cartledge, Heward, & Lo, 2006) and timely feedback and error correction (Cartledge & Kourea, 2008), as well as using culturally responsive classroom management (Cartledge, Lo, Vincent, & Robinson-Ervin, 2015) and building quality teacher student relationships (O'Connor, Dearing, & Collins, 2011) can all help students achieve academic success.

## Developing and/or Maintaining Cultural Competence

The lens through which educators choose to teach young children academic or social skills is just as critical as the skill itself. The learning experiences young children receive in their early years should expose them to a variety of racial, cultural, linguistic, and economic perspectives (Wright & Ford, 2017). A teacher's ability to draw upon the current familiarities of their students is integral to helping all students either develop or maintain cultural competence, which allows students to remain connected with their cultures while achieving academic excellence (Ladson-Billings, 1995). Teachers should make sure students from historically marginalized groups gain access to content and feel empowered (Hyland, 2010). For example, Wright and Ford (2017) assert that when students from diverse backgrounds feel a strong sense of in-group affiliation and identification with their race, it has an effect on their academic achievement. To ensure that this effect is positive, teachers should be equipped and intentional in their efforts to help students identify with individuals of the same race who demonstrate academic excellence.

Young children continuously internalize messages about race, gender, class, sexual orientation, and language (Hyland, 2010). The "residual effects of living in a racially stratified society do not escape children's detection" (Boutte, 2008, p. 167). Young children receive messages of discrimination from multiple sources (e.g., media, movies, television, books, home, peers). Counteracting these messages requires intense, targeted, and continuous efforts. In the classroom, it is critical that practices communicate and reinforce strong, subtle, and repeated social messages about what is and is not valued.

## Develop Critical Consciousness

The exploration of social justice issues can occur in multiple ways. Too often the presentation of an occasional literary text about a particular racial or ethnic group is insufficient for helping students develop or maintain cultural competency, as it communicates that diversity is an exception rather than the rule (Boutte, 2008).

Conversely, teachers can use children's literature to help make social issues around the world more concrete (Boutte, 2008). While engaging in conversations, rather than asking closed questions, teachers should ask pointed questions (e.g., questions of right and wrong, fairness, equity) so as to aid young children in thinking critically while challenging sources of power and ethnocentrism and thinking about their role in advocating for themselves or others.

## Culturally Responsive Teaching: How We Teach

Culturally responsive teaching (CRT) utilizes students' cultural knowledge, prior experiences, and performance styles as the launch pad for instructional design (Gay, 2010). The foundation for effective instruction in culturally responsive classrooms is empirically validated and relies on CRP (Gay, 2010). Research has revealed many instructional practices that are effective at increasing student achievement and decreasing problem behaviors in students from many marginalized groups. There is encouraging evidence that high-quality programs for young children of color can have lasting effects on cognitive and social skills (Conyers, Reynolds, & Ou, 2003). Although early childhood teachers play an important role in supporting healthy development of young children's social and emotional skills, research indicates that many early childhood educators are unaware of the evidence-based practices that can benefit students (Stormont, Reinke, & Herman, 2011). Culturally responsive practices—implemented while considering the academic, cultural, linguistic, and socioeconomic diversity of students—can be a powerful factor in addressing the opportunity gap.

## Evidence-Based Instructional Practices

**Selecting task difficulty.** When academic or behavioral problems arise in the classroom, one of the first factors to be examined should be whether instructional practices and materials are appropriate for the student (Center, Dietz, & Kaufman, 1982). Students are more likely to demonstrate increased on-task behavior, task completion, and task comprehension when assigned tasks are at the appropriate instructional level: neither too difficult nor too easy (Treptow et al., 2007; Umbreit et al., 2004). Early childhood educators should frequently monitor student success and failure on presented tasks and adjust difficulty accordingly. This will create a challenging environment with sufficient opportunities for individual student success.

Instructional level, defined as "a comfort zone created when the student has sufficient prior knowledge and skill to interact successfully with the task and still learn new information," (Gravois & Gickling, 2002, p. 888), can be affected by student beliefs developed through early experiences. CRT asserts that developmental appropriateness must also examine to what extent students enter school with negative beliefs about education that stem directly from racism (Brown-Jeffy & Cooper, 2011). Students of color, even at preschool age, may already have had experiences that devalued their worth based solely upon race, ethnicity, or culture, which, in turn, shapes their academic identity. Care must be taken by preschool teachers to understand the cultures of their students and to create culturally responsive classrooms that provide positive academic experiences for young children. This will, in turn, assist teachers to match the curricular materials and activities to the developmental level of students, keeping culture at the forefront and increasing the likelihood of early academic success.

**Opportunities for active responding.** Students who are deemed to be less capable have lower rates of academic responses in class (Good & Nichols, 2001). Because teachers often hold diminished views of the academic abilities of students of color (Pigott & Cowen, 2000), this could lead to fewer opportunities for these students to be actively engaged in class. It has been suggested that low rates of engagement can lead to students becoming anxious, withdrawn, and frustrated (Montague & Bergeron, 1997). Conversely, researchers have found that high rates of academic responding are associated with increases in correct student responses and reductions in disruptive behaviors for students of color in urban environments (Lambert et al., 2006). If students are exhibiting fewer behaviors that are seen as disruptive, the risk for special education referral or mental health evaluation may be lessened. In early educational settings, it is important to engage students in active responding as much as possible in order to assess for student understanding. Strategies that can be used to increase active student responding in young children include the use of choral responding and response boards or cards (Kern & Clemens, 2007). Further, evocative print referencing, which requires children to respond to teacher's questions about print, is frequently used with preschool children to increase engagement (Gettinger & Stoiber, 2014). Increased opportunities to respond not only have direct benefits for student engagement, they produce immediate data teachers can use to formatively assess student understanding.

**Timely feedback and error correction.** Increased opportunities to respond are useful only if students are providing accurate responses; if not, students are merely practicing mistakes. A hallmark of effective instruction is the provision of timely feedback, including error correction and positive reinforcement (Alber-Morgan,

Ramp, Anderson, & Martin, 2007; Chafouleas, Martens, Dobson, Weinstein, & Gardner, 2004). Error correction typically follows a set procedure; first, the teacher provides a corrective model following a student's incorrect academic response. Next, the student provides a correct response based on the teacher's model. During instruction, student mistakes must be immediately and explicitly corrected (Alber-Morgan et al., 2007). Positive reinforcement, both for effort toward improvement and for correct responding, must be promptly delivered to the student in order to increase the rate of future correct responding.

One promising intervention program that combines these strategies and others is the Behavioral, Emotional, and Social Training: Competent Learners Achieving School Success (BEST in CLASS; Conroy, Sutherland, Vo, Carr, & Ogston, 2014). BEST in CLASS supports early childhood educators' use of effective instructional practices that promote positive teacher-child interactions, increase student engagement and learning opportunities, and decrease problem behaviors (Vo, Sutherland, & Conroy, 2012).

## Evidence-Based Classroom Management

**Culturally responsive classroom management.** Weinstein, Tomlinson-Clarke, and Curran (2004) conceptualized five overarching principles that shape culturally responsive classroom management (CRCM): (1) recognition of teachers' own ethnocentrism, (2) knowledge of students' cultures, (3) understanding of the broader social, economic, and political systems in education, (4) appropriate management strategies, and (5) development of caring classrooms. Weinstein et al. (2004) stressed that CRCM is more than a set of predetermined skills, actions, and strategies that can be put into a manual and implemented by teachers; rather, teachers need to understand their own bias and be responsive to their students and classroom context.

While the population of U.S. schools is becoming increasingly diverse, the teaching force has remained homogenous; 82% white and 77% white women mostly from a middle-class socioeconomic background (Taie & Goldring, 2017). This cultural mismatch sets the occasion for teachers to misinterpret students' culturally specific behaviors. Further, children may have difficulty understanding the culture and behavioral expectations of the school (Gay & Howard, 2000). Culturally competent teachers take the time to learn about their students' cultures while examining their own biases. To be truly competent, teachers must recognize that their cultural norms are not absolute (Weinstein et al., 2004) and that culture dictates how we approach situations and react in social interactions (Cartledge et al., 2015).

One action teachers can take is to become critically reflective of how their beliefs and behaviors affect their teaching (Howard, 2003). For example, Howard (2003) suggests that critical reflection can take the form of responding to a series of pertinent questions, such as:

1. What is the racial or gender breakdown of the students that I typically send from my class for disciplinary action?
2. How often do I send the same students for disciplinary actions?
3. Do I dispense disciplinary referrals fairly on the basis of race and gender?
4. Are disciplinary actions therapeutic (teaching) or simply punitive?
5. Do I distinguish culturally specific behaviors from behavioral inadequacies?
6. If students have substantial behavioral differences, have I taught them the skills they need to know? Have I adequately practiced these skills to build fluency? Am I utilizing positive reinforcement when students display correct behavior? (p. 198)

CRCM also advocates for the use of preventative evidence-based classroom management techniques, implemented with fidelity (Weinstein et al., 2004) rather than the use of reactive punitive practices. Classroom management should promote behavioral self-regulation by students to enable them to take full advantage of available learning time (Skiba & Cummings, 2008). Some of the most effective of these practices are building relationships with students, establishing and teaching behavioral expectations, using error correction, and using contingent behavior-specific praise (BSP).

**Building relationships.** Classrooms with quality teacher-student relationships have been shown to have better academic performance and fewer problem behaviors (O'Connor et al., 2011). Conversely, negative teacher-student relationships predict limited school engagement, poor academic achievement, and problem behavior (Hamre & Pianta, 2001). Children in classrooms with more responsive teachers—those who are aware of and responsive to children's emotions, behaviors, and thoughts and make efforts to respond in supportive ways—make greater gains in early literacy, language, and working memory skills, while showing decreases in levels of teacher reported conflict (Hamre, Pianta, Hatfield, & Jamil, 2014). Among other characteristics, Ladson-Billings (1995) suggests culturally relevant teachers demonstrate connectedness with all students and develop a community of learners, as well as show students they care about them by holding all students to high expectations. Positive teacher-student relations appear to be especially important to students of color, as studies of these students' perceptions have repeatedly emphasized (Hollins & Spencer, 1990; Lee, 1999; Slaughter-Defoe & Carlson, 1996). Teachers can exhibit culturally connected caring by showing affection and nurturing behavior toward students (Howard, 2002).

**Establish and teach expectations.** Evidence suggests that cultural mismatch, societal stereotypes, and implicit bias may be to blame for disparities in discipline rates between African American and white students, especially for subjective offenses such as defiance and noncompliance (Gregory, Skiba, & Noguera, 2010). Differences in behavioral interpretations can be lessened by teachers using an authoritative style of teaching—one in which teachers demonstrate caring and high expectations (Gregory & Weinstein, 2008; Irvine, 2002). When teachers have a clear and explicit set of classroom expectations with corresponding behavioral expectations, they are anticipating problems and can promote more positive interactions in the classroom (Hardman & Smith, 1999). Furthermore, students of color may have less difficulty interpreting the verbal commands of teachers when expectations are explicitly taught and practiced. The most successful classrooms for all students are those in which high expectations are clearly stated, no excuses are permitted, and problem behaviors are handled immediately (Wilson & Corbett, 2001).

Each classroom routine (e.g., circle time, stations, free play, independent work, snack) should have specific expectations to assist transitions (Park & Lynch, 2014). The teacher must develop a system through which rules and routines are modeled, taught, and reinforced in consistent, positive, and structured ways (Lewis & Sugai, 1999). Teaching the rules and routines should include multiple examples, practice across multiple settings, and involvement of a variety of people (Lewis & Sugai, 1999). Making behavioral expectations transparent and providing opportunities for guided practice for all students in the classroom is the overarching goal of explicitly teaching and practicing rules and routines in this manner.

**Error correction.** As previously mentioned, students of color are more likely to be punished excessively for behaviors reflective of their culture and gender rather than taught appropriate replacement behaviors (U.S. Department of Education, 2016). Error corrections for social behaviors, also called explicit reprimands, are brief, concise statements that include the observed behavior and tell the student exactly what they should do in the future (Simonsen, Fairbanks, Briesch, Myers, & Sugai, 2008). In the preschool setting, perhaps more than other educational environments, teachers ought to assume that student behavioral errors are due to skill deficits and use error correction to assist in teaching appropriate social behaviors. Direct, immediate, explicit error corrections have the greatest effect on students' future success (Barbetta, Heward, Bradley, & Miller, 1994), and brevity and consistent delivery are more likely to facilitate student behavior change (Abramowitz, O'Leary, & Futtersak, 1988).

**Behavior specific praise (BSP).** Brophy (1981) determined that teacher praise was most effective when the teacher specified to the student the behavior being reinforced. Studies have repeatedly shown increases in prosocial behaviors parallel to increases in teachers' usage of BSP (Fullerton, Conroy, & Correa, 2009; Pisacreta, Tincani, Connell, & Axelrod, 2011; Stormont, Smith, & Lewis, 2007) and teachers who use more praise with their students experience fewer incidents of off-task and disruptive behaviors (Stormont & Reinke, 2009). Used proactively, BSP can stop many problem behaviors before they begin, even with the most challenging students (Stormont & Reinke, 2009). BSP reduces the need for reprimands and increases positive interactions with students (Reinke, Lewis-Palmer, & Merrell, 2008).

## Fostering Culturally Responsive Family Engagement

Especially during the critical early childhood period, family engagement is essential to foster child development and success. This is an essential component for supporting social emotional development. The first signs of emotional and behavioral risk in children will be evident in family or school environments and often across both; however, some children will show early problems in one setting and not the other. If proactive collaborative relationships are present across the multiple settings where children spend their time, then minor developmental challenges or more serious problems can be identified and supported through early intervention. Therefore, it is critical that professionals work to engage families through culturally responsive efforts.

When working with families of color, it is imperative that professionals capitalize on all of the strengths families have and harness these when working to prevent behavior problems. For example, teachers can invite family members to teach a lesson or provide guidance into the behavioral approaches used at home and within the child's culture. Too often families of color have had negative experiences within school and have been invited to meet with professionals when problems occur (Harniss, Epstein, Bursuck, Nelson, & Jayanthi, 2001; Hawes, 2008). Families may believe that professionals view their children and themselves from a risk lens rather than positive and additive lenses (McCoach et al., 2010; McDermott & Rothenberg, 2000).

Engaging families in their children's education benefits children and their families. Research has clearly found that children whose families are engaged in their school experience achieve more, have more positive social behavior and, in the end, graduate at higher rates (Barnard, 2004; Perna & Titus, 2005). An educator needs to build trust with families as a first step for engagement, while demonstrating competence as a teacher. Trust is formed when teachers communicate positively with families and children, reflecting personal interest in and acknowledgement of children's positive actions, strengths, talents, and behaviors in school.

When teachers form trusting relationships with parents and caregivers, they also demonstrate knowledge of and respect for families' characteristics, needs and strengths (Turnbull, Turnbull, Erwin, Soodak, & Shogren, 2011). To demonstrate respect for families, teachers must acknowledge what is important to each family member and communicate this knowledge. Respect for teachers occurs when families feel the teacher is competent and credible. This mutual respect is a necessary foundation for trusting relationships between teachers and family members. It is imperative that the foundational elements of forming partnerships with families are proactively extended to families of color.

## Proactive Family Engagement

"Part of the excitement of working in the field of education is to get a glimpse of the future of communities and the nation right in our classrooms […] Children in the classroom reflect the next generation and demonstrate the increasing diversity of America." (Grant & Ray, 2016, p. 134). One of the biggest barriers to effectively engaging families from diverse backgrounds is expecting all families to fit a similar mold of the "engaged parent = X," thus ignoring diverse perspectives and rich cultural differences. When teachers are working to engage families from cultures that are different from their own, they need to consider what engagement means in terms of their own beliefs and practices. For example, if cultural beliefs regarding teachers are that they should not be questioned and that families should not interfere with school practices, then families may seem uninvolved and apathetic toward school when, in fact, they do not want to be disrespectful to their children's teachers (Grant & Ray, 2016; Turnbull et al., 2011).

As an initial proactive step for engaging families, early childhood educators should consider defining family engagement in terms of what it means for their program or school. Educators can then work to achieve greater engagement by answering the following questions:

- In what ways can families be engaged?
- Are there specific families who may need extra support for participating, if they express they want to participate? (e.g., there may be barriers for families including childcare for other children, conflicting days of the week for work or religious practices, lack of transportation, etc.).
- How can we support family engagement?

Once these questions are explored, a parent support committee or group of families can be formed to help determine barriers to address and ways more families can be involved and engaged in their children's school experiences. Families could be presented with a wide array of options and could choose options that feel right for them and work for their schedules. These could include singing to a class or telling stories rather than reading a book, cooking treats for a class party in the school kitchen with supplies donated by others, or meeting at the library for parent-teaching meetings. The flexibility of these activities combined with the responsiveness to families' values and preferences can help support families' comfort in being more engaged in school.

**Understanding culture and promoting family engagement.** "Instead of viewing culture as a description of a group of people, perhaps a more useful approach for educators is to think of culture as the lens through which people view the world based on their backgrounds and experiences." (Grant & Ray, 2016, p. 137). Furthermore, individuals with various cultural backgrounds may identify with one culture more than another and, as individuals get older, they may change their views as their connections to different cultures change. Therefore, it is only through knowing families that educators can understand cultural factors that influence the way individuals view the world as well as beliefs and practices related to education.

When considering how to promote cultural understanding and engagement of different families, it is important for educators to explore unexamined biases and preconceived notions about family engagement. For example, and as mentioned previously in this article, there is often a mismatch between various cultural perspectives and the dominant culture. "Establishing respectful relationships with families of diverse cultures first involves understanding one's personal beliefs about culture and the complex nature of family engagement" (Grant & Ray, 2016, p. 140). Educators may also have rigid beliefs about what family engagement looks like. For example, some may believe that families should be partners with teachers in promoting learning in school settings, parents should support homework at home, and parents should be involved in other limited and teacher defined ways. All of these beliefs are barriers to promoting family engagement and must be adjusted when working with families of color.

# Summary

Children are most impressionable during the formative pre-school years. It is during these years that children begin to develop a sense of self and ascertain their place in their environment. Because of this, it is imperative that early childhood educators provide instruction that is culturally relevant in an environment that welcomes diverse families. Not only can early childhood experiences establish a base for academic success, they can counteract the detrimental messages children receive about human differences. Perhaps the solution to the well-documented achievement and opportunity gaps for students of color lies in the use of evidence-based, culturally relevant practices, and proactive family engagement by the first adults of influence in young children's educational career.

## References

Abramowitz, A. J., O'Leary, S. G., & Futtersak, M. W. (1988). The relative impact of long and short reprimands on children's off-task behavior in the classroom. *Behavior Therapy, 19*(2), 243–247. doi:10.1016/S0005-7894(88)80046-7

Adamu, M., & Hogan, L. (2015). *Point of entry: The preschool-to-prison pipeline.* Retrieved from https://cdn.americanprogress.org/wp-content/uploads/2015/10/08000111/PointOfEntry-reportUPDATE.pdf

Alber-Morgan, S. R., Matheson Ramp, E., Anderson, L. L., and Martin, C. (2007). Effects of repeated readings, error correction, and performance feedback on the fluency and comprehension of middle school students with behavior problems. *Journal of Special Education, 41*(1), 17–30.

Appleyard, K., Egeland, B., Dulmen, M. H., & Alan Sroufe, A. L. (2005). When more is not better: The role of cumulative risk in child behavior outcomes. *Journal of Child Psychology and Psychiatry, 46*(3), 235–245.

Barbetta, P. M., Heward, W. L., Bradley, D. M., & Miller, A. D. (1994). Effects of immediate and delayed error correction on the acquisition and maintenance of sight words by students with developmental disabilities. *Journal of Applied Behavior Analysis, 27*(1), 177–178.

Barnard, W. M. (2004). Parent involvement in elementary school and educational attainment. *Children and Youth Services Review, 26*(1), 39–62. doi:10.1016/j.childyouth.2003.11.002

Barnett, S., Carolan, M., & Johns, D. (2013). *Equity and excellence: African- American children's access to quality preschool.* New Brunswick, NJ: National Institute for Early Education Research.

Boutte, G. S. (2008). Beyond the illusion of diversity: How early childhood teachers can promote social justice. *Social Studies, 99*(4): 165–173.

Brody, G. H., Yi-Fu, C., Murry, V. M., Simons, R. L., Xiaojia, G., Gibbons, F. X., . . . Cutrona, C. E. (2006). Perceived discrimination and the adjustment of African American youths: A five-year longitudinal analysis with contextual moderation effects. *Child Development, 77*(5), 1170–1189.

Bronfenbrenner, U. (1994). Ecological models of human development. *International Encyclopedia of Education, 3*(2), 1643–1647.

Brophy, J. (1981). Teacher praise: A functional analysis. *Review of Educational Research, 51*(1), 5–32.

Brown-Jeffy, S., & Cooper, J. E. (2011). Toward a culturally relevant pedagogy: An overview of the conceptual and theoretical literature. *Teacher Education Quarterly, 38*(1), 65–84.

Cartledge, G., & Kourea, L. (2008). Culturally responsive classrooms for culturally diverse students with and at risk for disabilities. *Exceptional Children, 74*(3), 351–371.

Cartledge, G., Lo, Y. Y., Vincent, C. G., & Robinson-Ervin, P. (2015). Culturally responsive classroom management. In E. T. Emmer, & E. J. Sabornie (Eds.), *Handbook of classroom management* (2nd ed., pp. 411–430). New York, NY: Routledge.

Center, D. B., Dietz, S. M., & Kaufman, M. E. (1982). Student ability, task difficulty and inappropriate classroom behavior. *Behavior Modification, 6*, 335–375.

Chafouleas, S.M., Martens, B.K., Dobson, R.L., Weinstein, K.S. & Gardner, K.B. (2004). Fluent reading as the improvement of stimulus control: Additive effects of performance-based interventions to repeated reading on students' reading and error rates. *Journal of Behavioral Education, 13*(2), 67–81.

Cholewa, B., Goodman, R. D., West-Olatunji, C., & Amatea, E. (2014). A qualitative examination of the impact of culturally responsive educational practices on the psychological well-being of students of color. *Urban Review, 46*(4), 574–596.

Coie, J. D., Watt, N. F., West, S. G, Hawkins, J. D., Asarnow, J. R., Markman, H. J., …Long, B. (1993). The science of prevention: A conceptual framework and some directions for a national research program. *American Psychologist, 48*, 1013–1022.

Conroy, M. A., Sutherland, K. S., Vo, A. K., Carr, S., & Ogston, P. L. (2014). Early childhood teachers' use of effective instructional practices and the collateral effects on young children's behavior. *Journal of Positive Behavior Interventions, 16*(2), 81–92.

Conyers, L. M., Reynolds, A. J., & Ou, S. R. (2003). The effect of early childhood intervention and subsequent special education services: Findings from the Chicago Child-Parent Centers. *Educational Evaluation and Policy Analysis, 25*(1), 75–95.

Donovan, M. S., & Cross, C. T. (2002). *Minority students in special and gifted education.* Washington, D.C.: National Academies Press.

Dunlap, G., Strain, P. S., Fox, L., Carta, J. J., Conroy, M., Smith, B. J., . . . Sowell, C. (2006). Prevention and intervention with young children's challenging behavior: Perspectives regarding current knowledge. *Behavioral Disorders, 32*(1), 29–45.

Dunn, L. M. (1968). Special education for the mildly retarded: Is much of it justifiable? *Exceptional Children: Journal of the International Council for Exceptional Children, 35*(1), 5–22.

Edleson, J. L. (1999). Children's witnessing of adult domestic violence. *Journal of Interpersonal Violence, 14*(8), 839–870.

Fullerton, E. K., Conroy, M. A., & Correa, V. I. (2009). Early childhood teachers' use of specific praise statements with young children at risk for behavioral disorders. *Behavioral Disorders, 34*(3), 118–135.

Gay, G. (2010). *Culturally responsive teaching theory, research, and practice* (2nd ed.). New York, NY: Teachers College Press.

Gay, G., & Howard, T. C. (2000). Multicultural teacher education for the 21st century. *The Teacher Educator, 36*(1), 1–16.

Gay, G. (2013). Teaching to and through cultural diversity. *Curriculum Inquiry, 43*(1), 48–70.

Good, T. L., & Nichols, S. L. (2001). Expectancy effects in the classroom: A special focus on improving the reading performance of minority students in first-grade classrooms. *Educational Psychologist, 36*(2), 113–126.

Goodman, R. D., & West-Olatunji, C. A. (2010). Educational hegemony, traumatic stress, and African American and Latino American students. *Journal of Multicultural Counseling and Development, 38*, (176–186).

Grant, K. B., & Ray, J. (2016). *Home, school, and family collaboration: Culturally responsive family engagement* (3rd ed). Thousand Oakes, CA: SAGE.

Gettinger, M. & Stoiber, K.C. (2014). Increasing opportunities to respond to print during storybook reading: Effects of evocative print-referencing techniques. *Early Childhood Research Quarterly, 28*(3), 283–297.

Gravois, T. A., & Gickling, E. E. (2002). Best practices in curriculum-based assessment. In A. Thomas & J. Grimes (Eds.), *Best practices in school psychology IV* (pp. 885–898). Washington, DC: National Association of School Psychologists.

Green, A. L., & Stormont, M. (2017). Creating culturally responsive and evidence-based lesson plans for students of color with disabilties. *Intervention in School and Clinic, 53*(3), 138–145.

Gregory, A., Skiba, R. J., & Noguera, P. A. (2010). The achievement gap and the discipline gap: Two sides of the same coin? *Educational Researcher, 39*(1), 59–68.

Gregory, A., & Weinstein, R. S. (2008). The discipline gap and African Americans: Defiance or cooperation in the high school classroom. *Journal of School Psychology, 46*, 455–475.

Hamre, B. K., & Pianta, R. C. (2001). Early teacher–child relationships and the trajectory of children's school outcomes through eighth grade. *Child Development, 72*(2), 625–638. doi:10.1111/1467-8624.00301

Hamre, B., Hatfield, B., Pianta, R., & Jamil, F. (2014). Evidence for general and domain-specific elements of teacher–child interactions: Associations with preschool children's development. *Child Development, 85*(3), 1257–1274.

Hardman, E., & Smith, S. W. (1999). Promoting positive interactions in the classroom. *Intervention in School and Clinic, 34*(3), 178–180.

Harniss, M. K., Epstein, M. H., Bursuck, W. D., Nelson, J., & Jayanthi, M. (2001). Resolving homework-related communication problems: Recommendations of parents of children with and without disabilities. *Reading & Writing Quarterly, 17*, 205–225.

Hawes, K. (2008). Parents are not the enemy: Ten tips for improving parent teacher communication. *Mathematics Teacher, 101*, 328–331.

Hay, D. F., Pawlby, S., Angold, A., Harold, G. T., & Sharp, D. (2003). Pathways to violence in the children of mothers who were depressed postpartum. *Developmental Psychology, 39*(6), 1083.

Heller, K. A., Holtzman, W. H., & Messick, S. (1982). *Placing children in special education: A strategy for equity.* Washington, D.C.: National Academy Press.

Hollins, E. R., & Spencer, K. (1990). African American and Latino children in high-poverty urban schools: How they perceive school climate. *Journal of Negro Education, 65*(1), 60–70.

Howard, T. C. (2003). Culturally relevant pedagogy: Ingredients for critical teacher reflection. *Theory into Practice, 42*(3), 195–202.

Howard, T.C. (2002). Hearing footsteps in the dark: African American students' descriptions of effective teachers. *Journal of Education for Students Placed at Risk, 7*(4), 425–444.

Hyland, N. E. (2010). Social justice in the early childhood classrooms: What the research tells us. *YC Young Children, 65*(1), 82.

Irvine, J. J. (2002). *In search of wholeness: African American teachers and their culturally competent classroom practices.* New York, NY: Palgrave.

Irvine, J. J. (2012). Complex relationships between multicultural education and special education: An African American perspective. *Journal of Teacher Education, 63*(4), 268–274.

Kauffman, J. M., & Landrum, T. J. (2013). *Characteristics of emotional and behavioral disorders of children and youth* (10th ed.). Upper Saddle River, NJ: Pearson Education.

Kern, L., & Clemens, N. H. (2007). Antecedent strategies to promote appropriate classroom behavior. *Psychology in the Schools, 44*(1), 65–75.

Knitzer, J., and Lefkowitz. J. (2006). Helping the most vulnerable infants, toddlers, and their families. Pathways to Early School Success, Issue Brief no. 1. New York, NY: *National Center for Children in Poverty*, Columbia University.

Ladson-Billings, G. (1995). Toward a theory of culturally relevant pedagogy. *American Educational Research Journal, 32*(3), 465–491.

Lambert, M. C., Cartledge, G., Heward, W. L., & Lo, Y. Y. (2006). Effects of response cards on disruptive behavior and academic responding during math lessons by fourth-grade urban students. *Journal of Positive Behavior Interventions, 8*(2), 88–99.

Lee, P. W. (1999). In their own voices: An ethnographic study of low-achieving students within the context of school reform. *Urban Education, 34*(2), 214–244.

Lewis, T. J., & Sugai, G. (1999). Effective behavior support: A systems approach to proactive schoolwide management. *Focus on Exceptional Children, 31*(6), 1–24.

McCoach, D., Goldstein, J., Behuniak, P., Reis, S. M., Black, A. C., Sullivan, E. E., & Rambo, K. (2010). Examining the unexpected: Outlier analyses of factors affecting student achievement. *Journal of Advanced Academics, 21*, 426–468. doi:10.1177/1932202X1002100304

McDermott, P., & Rothenberg, J. (2000). Why urban parents resist involvement in their children's elementary education. *The Qualitative Report, 5*(3), 1–16. Retrieved from http://nsuworks.nova.edu/tqr/vol5/iss3/4/

McMiller, W. P., Weisz, J. R. (1996). Help-seeking preceding mental health clinic intake among African-American, Latino, and Caucasian youths. *Journal of the American Academy of Child & Adolescent Psychiatry, 35*(8), 1086–1094.

Montague, M., & Bergeron, J. (1997). Using prevention strategies in general education. *Focus on Exceptional Children, 29,* 1–12.

Niesyn, M. E. (2009). Strategies for success: Evidence-based instructional practices for students with emotional and behavioral disorders. *Preventing School Failure: Alternative Education for Children and Youth, 53*(4), 227–234.

O'Connor, E. E., Dearing, E., & Collins, B. A. (2011). Teacher-child relationship and behavior problem trajectories in elementary school. *American Educational Research Journal, 48*(1), 120–162.

Oswald, D. P., Coutinho, M. J., Best, A. M., & Singh, N. N. (1999). Ethnic representation in special education: The influence of school-related economic and demographic variables. *The Journal of Special Education, 32*(4), 194–206.

Park, H.-S. L., & Lynch, S. A. (2014). Evidence-based practices for addressing classroom behavior problems. *Young Exceptional Children, 17*(3), 33–47. doi:10.1177/1096250613496957

Perna, L., & Titus, M. (2005). The relationship between parental involvement as social capital and college enrollment: An examination of racial/ethnic group differences. *The Journal of Higher Education, 76*(5), 485–518.

Pigott, R.L., & Cowen, E.L. (2000). Teacher race, child race, racial congruence, and teacher ratings of children's school adjustment. *Journal of School Psychology, 38,* 177–195. http://dx.doi.org/10.1016/S0022-4405(99)00041-2.

Pires, S. A., Grimes, K.E., Allen, K.D., Gilmer, T., & Mahadevan, R. M. (2013). *Examining children's behavioral health service utilization and expenditures.* Hamilton, N.J.: Center for Health Care Strategies, Inc.

Pisacreta, J., Tincani, M., Connell, J. E., & Axelrod, S. (2011). Increasing teachers' use of a 1:1 praise-to-behavior correction ratio to decrease student disruption in general education classrooms. *Behavioral Interventions, 26*(4), 243–260.

Reinke, W. M., Lewis-Palmer, T., & Merrell, K. (2008). The classroom check-up: A classwide teacher consultation model for increasing praise and decreasing disruptive behavior. *School Psychology Review, 37*(3), 315–332.

Romero, A. J., Martinez, D., & Carvajal, S. C. (2007). Bicultural stress and adolescent risk behaviors in a community sample of Latinos and non-Latino European Americans. *Ethnicity and Health, 12,* 443–463.

Scott, T.M., & Barrett, S.B. (2004). Using staff and student time engaged in disciplinary procedures to evaluate the impact of school-wide PBS. *Journal of Positive Behavior Interventions, 6,* 21–27.

Shonkoff, J. P., Boyce, W. T., Cameron, J., Duncan, G. J., Fox, N. A., & Greenough, W. T. (2004). *Children's emotional development is built into the architecture of their brains.* Cambridge, MA: National Scientific Council on the Developing Child.

Simonsen, B., Fairbanks, S., Briesch, A., Myers, D., & Sugai, G. (2008). Evidence-based practices in classroom management: Considerations for research to practice. *Education and Treatment of Children, 31*(3), 351–380.

Skiba, R. J., Albrecht, S. F., & Losen, D. J. (2013). CCBD's position summary on federal policy on disproportionality in special education. *Behavioral Disorders, 38*(2),108–120.

Skiba, R. J., Simmons, A. B., Ritter, S., Gibb, A. C., Rausch, M. K., Cuadrado, J., & Chung, C. (2008). Achieving equity in special education: History, status, and current challenges. *Exceptional Children, 74*(3), 264–288.

Skiba, R., & Cummings, J. (2008). *Interventions for classroom disruption: Addressing emotional and behavioral problems in the classroom.* Washington, DC: American Psychological Association.

Slaughter-Defoe, D. T., & Carlson, K. G. (1996). Young African American and Latino children in high-poverty urban schools: How they perceive school climate. *Journal of Negro Education, 65*(1), 60–70.

Stormont, M., & Reinke, W. (2009). The importance of precorrective statements and behavior-specific praise and strategies to increase their use. *Beyond Behavior, 18*(3), 26–32.

Stormont, M., Reinke, W., & Herman, K. (2011). Teachers' knowledge of evidence-based interventions and available school resources for children with emotional and behavioral problems. *Journal of Behavioral Education, 20*(2), 138–147.

Stormont, M. A., Smith, S. C., & Lewis, T., J. (2007). Teacher implementation of precorrection and praise statements in Head Start classrooms as a component of a program-wide system of positive behavior support. *Journal of Behavioral Education, 16*(3), 280. doi:10.1007/s10864-007-9040-3

Sullivan, A. L., Van Norman, E. R., & Klingbeil, D. A. (2014). Exclusionary discipline of students with disabilities: Student and school characteristics predicting suspension. *Remedial and Special Education, 35*(4), 199–210.

Taie, S., and Goldring, R. (2017). *Characteristics of Public Elementary and Secondary School Teachers in the United States: Results From the 2015–16 National Teacher and Principal Survey First Look* (NCES 2017–072). U.S. Department of Education. Washington, DC: National Center for Education Statistics.

Townsend, B. L. (2000). The disproportionate discipline of African American learners: Reducing school suspensions and expulsions. *Exceptional Children, 66*(3), 381–391.

Treptow, M. A., Burns, M. K., & McComas, J. J. (2007). Reading at the frustration, instructional, and independent levels: The effects on students' reading comprehension and time on task. *School Psychology Review, 36*(1), 159.

Turnbull, A., Turnbull, R., Erwin, E., Soodak, L., & Shogren, K. A. (2011). *Families, professionals, and exceptionality: Positive outcomes through partnerships and trust*. Upper Saddle River, NJ: Pearson.

U.S. Department of Education Office for Civil Rights. (2014). *Civil Rights Data Collection*. Retrieved from ocrdata.ed.gov/

U.S. Department of Education (2016). *A first look: Key data highlights on equity and opportunity gaps in our nation's public schools*. Washington, D.C.: U.S. Department of Education.

Umbreit, J., Lane, K. L., & Dejud, C. (2004). Improving classroom behavior by modifying task difficulty: Effects of increasing the difficulty of too-easy tasks. *Journal of Positive Behavior Interventions, 6*(1), 13–20.

Vanneman, A., Hamilton, L., Baldwin Anderson, J., & Rahman, T. (2009). *Achievement gaps: How black and white students in public schools perform in mathematics and reading on the national assessment of educational progress*. Washington, D.C.: National Center for Education Statistics, Institute of Education Sciences, U.S. Department of Education.

Vo, A. K., Sutherland, K. S., & Conroy, M. A. (2012). Best in class: A classroom-based model for ameliorating problem behavior in early childhood settings. *Psychology in the Schools, 49*(5), 402–415.

Walker, K. (2011). Deficit thinking and the effective teacher. *Education & Urban Society, 43*, 576–597.

Weinstein, C.S.., Tomlinson-Clarke, S., & Curran, M. (2004). Toward a conception of culturally responsive classroom management. *Journal of Teacher Education, 55*(1), 25–38.

Wells, R., Hillemeier, M. M., Bai, Y., & Belue, R. (2009). Health service access across racial/ethnic groups of children in the child welfare system. *Child Abuse & Neglect, 33*(5), 282–292.

Wilson, B. L., & Corbett, H. D. (2001). *Listening to urban kids: School reform and the teachers they want*. Albany, NY: State University of New York Press.

Wright, B. L., & Ford, D. Y. (2017). Untapped potential: Recognition of giftedness in early childhood and what professionals should know about students of color. *Gifted Child Today, 40*(2), 111–116.

# First Step Next: An Updated Version of the First Step to Success Early Intervention Program

*Hill Walker, Edward G. Feil, Andy Frey, Jason Small, John Seeley, Annemieke Golly, Shantel Crosby, Jon Lee, Steve Forness, Marilyn Sprick, Cristy Coughlin, and Brianna Stiller*

## Abstract

This manuscript describes a major revision and update of the First Step to Success Early Intervention Program, now called First Step Next. The original First Step Program was published in 1997 and the revised, updated version was published in 2015 (Walker et al.). First Step Next is a collaborative, Tier II school- and family-supported early intervention that teaches school success skills to give students the best start possible in their school career. This manuscript covers five major topics: (1) program history, (2) rationale and procedures for the First Step revision, (3) First Step Next implementation, (4) maintenance and follow up procedures, and (5) current and future research on First Step Next.

Keywords: First Step, intervention, education, Tier II, First Step Next, revision, update

The First Step to Success Program (Walker, et al., 1997) is a Tier II early intervention designed specifically for K–3 students who bring challenging or disruptive behavior patterns to the schooling experience. It is founded on the prevention science knowledge base (Pennington, 2002) and is a collaborative school-home intervention. The original First Step school-home intervention included (a) one-to-one instruction from a behavioral coach in school success skills, (b) ongoing opportunities and feedback provided to facilitate mastery of these skills in classroom and playground contexts, (c) a home component where parents learned to teach and support school success skills in the home context, and (d) use of group and individual contingencies at school and home respectively to facilitate skill acquisition and sustainability of achieved gains. First Step Next involves a cooperative arrangement among parents, teachers, peers and a behavioral coach, which lasts approximately three months and teaches social skills and academic enablers focused on supporting school success.

The original First Step program is set up and operated initially by a behavioral coach who then gradually turns over its daily operation to the cooperating teacher. The coach provides supervision and troubleshooting support to the teacher for the remainder of the three-month implementation period. The program's components are gradually faded out as part of the implementation schedule until the focus student's gains are supported by the intrinsic reinforcements of enhanced academic and social performance and positive feedback and praise from the teacher, parents, peers and coach. The purpose of this manuscript is to describe a substantial revision and update of the original First Step Program, as described above, to highlight essential features of the updated First Step Next Intervention, and to profile current and future research efforts.

## Program History

First Step was originally created through a model development grant from the U.S. Office of Special Education programs to the senior author of this paper. The grant ran from 1992 to 1996. Over the ensuing 20 years, following its initial development, a robust evidence base has developed around the First Step Program, consisting of a mix of single case studies and randomized controlled trials involving both efficacy and effectiveness studies. This evidence is reviewed extensively by Walker et al. (2014).

First Step has been the focus of four randomized controlled trials (RCT) that have produced impressive effect sizes on behavioral, social and even some academic outcome measures (Feil et al., 2014; Frey, Small et al., 2013; Walker et al., 2009; Walker, Golly, McLane, &

Kimmich, 2005). There has also been a national, five-site RCT that demonstrated its effectiveness with limited involvement by the program's developers (Sumi et al., 2013; Woodbridge et al., 2014). As part of this process, the First Step parent component was enhanced through the addition of motivational interviewing, technical and empirical knowledge (Frey, Lee et al., 2013). In addition, subsample analyses of these studies have produced evidence for First Step's success with children at risk for ADHD (Feil et al., 2016; Seeley et al., 2009); autism (Frey et al., 2015); and, at least partially, anxiety disorders (Seeley et al., in press). There has also been a separate, successful RCT for tertiary-level students (Frey, Small et al., 2015). Multiple studies have consistently shown positive effects on a full range of outcomes including teacher and parent reports as well as direct observation.

In addition, the program meets Flay et al.'s (2005) criteria for indicators of efficacy, effectiveness, and readiness for dissemination (Walker et al., 2014). First Step has also been reviewed and recognized by the What Works Clearinghouse of the U.S. Department of Education as a promising intervention. It is worth noting that First Step to date has been applied successfully with over 2,000 behaviorally at-risk students in the preschool and primary grade ranges. The program has been translated into Spanish and has been adopted and implemented successfully in the following countries other than the U.S.: Canada, Australia, New Zealand, Holland, Norway, Indonesia, and Turkey.

## Rationale and Procedures for the First Step Revision

The revision team's efforts were guided by three core principles: (1) to standardize the First Step Program components and forge them into a single unified module; (2) to make the program more user-friendly for implementers, including parents; and (3) to increase the program's efficacy by adding new components and updating existing ones. An important issue considered in initiating this yearlong process was that, over two decades of adoption and implementation, the program had undergone a number of innovations and adaptations by different implementers, resulting in competing versions of the original intervention being circulated among end users.

Further, through a program of troubleshooting and technical assistance efforts, the team received important feedback from numerous implementers regarding certain recurring challenges. One was that parents and some teachers felt the program required too much time and effort to justify the gains achieved, leading to lowered implementation fidelity and reduced program acceptance. A second criticism was that First Step coaches needed more detailed information on student behavioral characteristics and academic skills to individualize the program successfully. Third, implementers commented that the coach phase of the program needed to expand to provide younger students increased opportunities to acquire the new skills taught. This anecdotal information was derived from hundreds of First Step implementations and proved invaluable in helping guide the revision process that resulted in First Step Next. By maintaining a qualitative archive of this feedback, the team was able to see recurring patterns of implementation and structural issues that needed addressing in a revision. It also indicated a need for certain changes in program content. Go to http://www.firststeptosuccess.org/ to access documents produced by this research and for more detailed program information about First Step.

The First Step revision team consisted of a subset of the original First Step Program authors (Walker, Stiller, Golly, and Feil) along with the addition of two new members (Marilyn Sprick and Cristy Coughlin of Pacific Northwest Publishing). This group met regularly for a year to plan and carry out the revision.

## Differences Between Original First Step and the Updated First Step Next Program

The revision process that resulted in the updated version of First Step preserved the core elements of the original program that most account for its efficacy (i.e., direct instruction in school success skills, group and individual contingencies, peer and home support, school and home reward activities, and a dense schedule of positive feedback and descriptive praise). A number of the original procedures were identical, revised or only slightly updated. Overall, the First Step Next revision team's goal was to make the program more streamlined, less complex, and easier to implement with integrity. At present, the group is evaluating whether First Step Next appears to be more acceptable to consumers (i.e., perceived as less work by cooperating teachers and parents) than the original version, as described in the "Current Research" section. First Step Next now covers the pre-K through Grade 2 student population with only one program, whereas the original First Step program covered grades K-3 and relied on a separate preschool version to handle earlier developmental stages.

A fundamental difference between original First Step and First Step Next is that the latter is a more curricular-based intervention with a stronger instructional focus accompanied by a behavior-management component that provides incentives for the student to master and demonstrate the program's Super Student Skills, while simultaneously fostering adherence to the teacher's classroom rules. The original First Step Program was primarily a behavioral intervention with much more of a developmental focus. First Step Next by design has a more balanced academic and social-emotional emphasis, as the team received feedback from many teachers that academic readiness was also a strong priority for early intervention. Thus, it was decided to revise the First Step skills list to incorporate academic readiness skills as well as academic enablers to address this concern. Aside from improving overall First Step Next outcomes, it was felt that this change would make the program more acceptable to end users. Specific details regarding the Super Student Skills are provided below under "Changes in First Step Structure, Content, and Delivery."

In order to address the above revision goals, the team selected two broad program areas for concentration: (a) pre-implementation procedures and resources and (b) the structure, content and delivery of the First Step Program.

## Changes in Pre-Implementation

One of the takeaway lessons from the team's long-term experience with First Step implementation across a diverse set of school contexts was that Tier II programs such as First Step which focus on individual students are less effective when applied within chaotic classrooms. We found that not addressing classroom contextual problems prior to implementation consistently produced less robust First Step outcomes than expected. First Step Next now includes added features designed to address this important challenge by assessing classroom climate and expectations and evaluating students based on the program's Super Student Skills. These measures allow the coach to judge whether the classroom has a difficult management context that would deter implementation of First Step Next. In this event, the teacher is provided with lessons, resources and coaching guidance/support for teaching four important classroom expectations: (a) when the teacher needs your attention, look and listen; (b) stay in your personal space with hands and feet to yourself; (c) walk in the classroom; and (d) use a classroom voice. Under the coach's supervision, a five-step instructional procedure to teach these behavioral expectations to the whole class is shared with the teacher. Following completion of this task, the First Step Next program is then implemented with the focus student.

Another change in pre-implementation involved the screening procedures used to identify focus students. Originally, First

Step screening consisted of extensive teacher ratings and in vivo behavioral observations. These procedures in First Step Next now include a reduced number of academic-engaged time observations along with brief teacher ratings of oppositional-aggressive behavior as well as the teacher's judgment of the focus student's status on the super skills list. An optional Functional Behavioral Assessment is also included as part of the screening process.

## Changes in First Step Structure, Content, and Delivery

Perhaps the most essential addition to First Step Next is the Super Student Skills. First Step Next teaches mastery of a set of discrete social-emotional skills and academic-enabling skills: (a) follow directions, (b) be safe, (c) ask for help the right way, (d) be a team player, (e) do your best work, (f) be cool, and (g) mistakes are okay. Academic enablers are forms of social behavior that facilitate academic performance (i.e. focusing attention, accepting teacher corrections, engaging with assigned tasks, and cooperating with other students; DiPerna, 2006). Mastery of these skills contributes to school success as defined by both academic competence and social-emotional adjustment.

These skills are systematically taught in First Step Next by the teacher and coach, using lesson plans that label, define and describe each skill's purpose. Appendix A provides a skills list and accompanying narrative text to illustrate each of these features. Each First Step Next focus student also has a Super Skills workbook.

The coach phase of First Step Next is expanded from 5 to 7 program days depending on the focus student's progress and the cooperating teacher's judgment. Younger students tend to benefit from a longer coach phase. Program days 8–10 involve transfer of control and management of the program to the teacher, who assumes full program operation on day 11. The daily operation of First Step Next initially focuses on the teacher's classroom rules with bonus points and praise awarded for reinforcing the focus student's display of the target Super Student Skills as they are being taught. These discrete skills are introduced, role played, taught, and strengthened by the coach and teacher during the program's ongoing operation with home support provided by parents.

Substantial changes were made regarding the parents' role in the First Step Next intervention. Specifically, the original parent involvement procedures, called homeBase, consisted of six home visits by the First Step behavioral coach. Using a parent handbook combined with modeling, demonstration, and role plays, the coach instructed the focus child's parents on how to teach the school success skills at home. The child's teacher then looked for, prompted, and reinforced the skills' display at school. Although many of the parent engagement activities, such as phone calls, provision of home rewards, and daily check-in notes were retained, the home-Base component has been eliminated in First Step Next. Instead, parents are given an orientation to the First Step Next program and their roles in it prior to implementation. Close contact between the coach, teacher, and parents during implementation affords parents the opportunity to continue learning about the program and their role in it. Parents are also provided with a workbook that describes home activities and strategies they can use to help ensure the child's school success. In the updated program, the parents' daily tasks are extended to cover the full implementation period of 20 program days.

The rationale for this program change was two-fold. First, the team found some parents had difficulty teaching homeBase skills to their children, due to factors such as insufficient time and lack of motivation. Second, outcome data suggested somewhat lower effect sizes for parent ratings of child outcomes, as opposed to teacher ratings. For these reasons, parents were relieved of directly teaching the First Step Next Super Student Skills at home. That task now becomes the joint responsibility of the coach and teacher at school. Parents are still involved in First Step Next program implementation. However, a major emphasis for parents is to continue positive interactions with their child at home and to support strongly the child's continuing school progress. If the parents seem ready and request more information on effective parenting skills, the First Step coach also makes this material available to them. The family materials folder includes a home and school connections workbook for parents, a Super Student coloring book, and Super Student lesson cards.

In addition, a more formal debriefing component, immediately following problem situations, has been added to the First Step Next program. In this procedure the focus student and the coach review problems and examine how they played out, with input from the teacher as appropriate. The goal is for the focus student to realize how she or he could have handled the problem situation differently. This procedure is followed on a daily basis initially, and then used through the remainder of implementation based on need. Early on in the program, it is critical that the First Step Next student gets to review how difficult situations could have been handled better. Using a problem-solving process, the focus student is guided in developing positive behavioral alternatives. As a general rule, First Step focus students are not skilled in coming up with adaptive alternatives as to how they might behave differently in problem situations. These self-regulatory strategies have shown considerable promise with students that have emotional or behavioral disorders (Menzies, Lane, & Lee, 2009).

Finally, First Step Next includes different and more robust maintenance options and troubleshooting procedures, new demonstration videos, and a CD-ROM containing program materials that can be reproduced including downloadable training presentations, forms, checklists, and measures. A training DVD is also provided that models correct procedures for conducting parent and teacher meetings for the coach, Super Student Skills teaching lessons, and a teaching session with the class as a whole (see Walker et al., 2015).

## First Step Next Implementation

As can be seen in Table 1, the intervention consists of three major tasks, including social skills instruction, the Green Card game, and school-home connections. These tasks are addressed across four implementation phases (preparation, coach, teacher, and maintenance). The coach coordinates these tasks in collaboration with the focus student as well as the student's parents, peers, and teachers. The primary goal of instruction is to introduce, model, practice, and role-play the seven Super Student Skills: follow directions, be safe, ask for attention the right way, be a team player, do your best, be cool, and mistakes are okay. Coaches initially teach these skills in one-on-one sessions with the focus student. The coach also teaches the focus student about the Green Card game, which has green on one side and red on the other. The card provides positive feedback to the student for following teacher expectations (green side visible) and non-verbal negative feedback when the student does not comply with teacher expectations (red side visible). The coach operates the card initially and then turns it over to the teacher, who wears it on a lanyard around his or her neck for easy display. Students are taught that when the green side of the card is visible, they are doing well, and should keep it up. When they see the red side, they should "stop, think, and get back on track." An optional whole-class version of social-skills instruction can also be used.

The Green Card game is played with all the children in the focus student's class. Other students are taught to help the focus student keep the card on green. Points are awarded to the focus student for keeping the card on green; when 80% or more of the available daily points are earned while the green side of the card is showing, a brief, socially-rewarding activity or game involving the focus student and peers occurs immediately. A daily home note communicates results of the game to the parents, who reinforce this success with an individual activity/reward as soon as the child returns home. If the criterion is not met, that program day is repeated and/or an earlier, successfully completed program day is scheduled before proceeding.

If the daily performance criterion is not met for three consecutive days, modifications are made according to the needs of the child (often in coach consultation with the child, teacher, and parent). These can include changing rewards and adjusting the reinforcement system and the intensity of attention required.

**Table 1.**
*First Step Next Implementation Phases and Tasks*

| Tasks | Implementation Phases | | | | |
|---|---|---|---|---|---|
| | Preparation | Coach | Teacher | Maintenance | Next year follow up |
| **Social skill instruction** | Meet with student, discuss rewards | Conduct Super Student lessons, model with green card | Review Super Student Skills as necessary | Review Super Student Skills as necessary | Reintroduce Super Student Skills, Focus student: 5 lessons, Entire class: 4 lessons |
| **Green Card game** | Observations, teacher meeting | Play Green Card game day 1–7 | Play Green Card game days 8–20 | Play Green Card game days 21–30+ | Play Green Card game with focus student days 1–5 Play Green Card game with entire class days 6–20 |
| **Home-school connection** | Parent, teacher, coach meeting | Daily notes, daily phone calls | Daily notes, weekly phone-calls | If still playing with focus child- take daily notes | Daily graduate notes home, daily phone calls |

Initially, coaches directly implement the program for brief portions of the school day and also monitor, supervise, and support participating teachers as they assume control of the program. As the First Step Next Program is fully implemented, it is gradually extended to the full school day. It is important to note that spending the extra time to ensure that the child, parents and teacher all share the same understanding and expectations is essential for First Step success, particularly given that many of the focus children are from low-income, diverse neighborhoods in which culturally responsive procedures are especially critical (Council for Children with Behavior Disorders, 2013).

School-home connection activities and resources (i.e., meetings, school-home notes, and a parent workbook) are designed to help parents reinforce the student's successful use of the Super Student Skills. Parents are taught to use positive parenting strategies that help students apply Super Student Skills in the home setting as well as at school.

## Maintenance and Follow-up Procedures

First Step Next now includes maintenance procedures intended to provide needed ongoing behavioral support to the focus student during the remainder of the school year as well as follow up into the next school year to effect a seamless transition between grades. Research to date has convincingly shown that short-term behavioral interventions such as First Step should contain a follow-up maintenance plan to preserve achieved behavioral gains both within the remainder of the implementation school year and into the following school year (Sumi et al., 2013; Woodbridge et al., 2014). If possible, focus students should be followed, monitored and supported in subsequent school years to sustain program gains. To achieve this goal with First Step Next, the team has designed a next year follow-up plan, which contains a reduced variation of the full First Step Next implementation. Specifically, the next year follow-up maintenance activities include an initial meeting with the focus student and new teacher, social skills instruction, and the explanation-demonstration of the Green Card game to the focus student and peers. For the meeting with the focus student, the coach reviews the First Step Next intervention and solicits the child's understanding of the Green Card game, describes the next year follow-up procedures, and gets the student's ideas for how the two of them could best teach the Green Card game and Super Student Skills to the entire class. The social-skills instruction provided is similar to that which occurred during the previous year; daily social-skills instruction is implemented for a minimum of five days, and as needed thereafter. Social-skills lessons last between 5 and 15 minutes.

The coach coordinates the roles of parents, peers and the new teacher in order to sustain program gains and to provide needed supports and assistance to the focus student. The coach calls the parents during each of the first 5 days of the next year's maintenance plan, and completes and sends home the daily school-home connection note. After turning the maintenance program's operation over to the new teacher, the coach strongly encourages the teacher to continue with daily connection notes for the focus student and to use the generic school-home note with other students as needed. It is highly recommended that the coach and teacher jointly sustain these maintenance procedures during the remainder of the follow-up school year, if possible.

## Current Research on First Step Next

Currently, the First Step Next research team is conducting two Institute of Education Sciences (IES) Goal 3 studies with First Step Next. The first study provides an opportunity to examine several different outcomes of the intervention along with extensive data on consumer satisfaction and teacher-coach alliance. One of these projects focuses on preschool and the other is a comparative effectiveness study with tertiary-level, K–3 students that examines the impact of First Step Next, when delivered alone and in combination with a positive parenting intervention, compared to a control condition. Both projects are 4-year RCTs currently at their midpoint (Grant # R324Al50221—Preschool First Step to Success: An Efficacy Replication; and Grant # R324Al50l79—First Step Next and homeBase Comparative Efficacy Study).

## Preschool Replication Study

This 4-year RCT compares First Step Next with a usual care condition. The purpose of the study is to conduct a Goal 3 efficacy study of First Step Next to replicate the positive effects previously achieved with the preschool version of the First Step intervention in improving social-behavioral and academically-related outcomes and to assess the intervention's utility for preschool applications (Feil et al., 2014).

A diverse group of preschool teachers and parents in Oregon, Kentucky, and Illinois consented to be involved in this study. This IES Goal 3 project will provide the foundation for a future effectiveness study by demonstrating (a) efficacy, supported by at least two rigorous trials; (b) specific intervention enhancements available for training and supervision; and (c) measurement and design features to test the program's impact at a broader site level rather than at just the classroom level. Pre-, post-, immediate follow-up, and one-year follow-up data are currently being collected in this study. The team is using a cluster-randomized controlled trial design that nests teachers and classrooms within early childhood sites, with 58 sites involving 174 low-income families having preschoolers who meet inclusion criteria and who agreed to participate in the study.

## First Step Next and homeBase Efficacy Study

The second study, as noted, focuses on young elementary-age children (K-3) and appears to be one of the first comparative effec-tiveness studies to be attempted in a multi-tiered framework. It involves tertiary-level children with severe emotional and behavioral problems and its feasibility has been supported in a recent preliminary study. This is also an IES-funded Goal 3 study, currently near its midpoint.

In this RCT, the team's interest is in directly comparing the First Step Next classroom-based intervention with the homeBase intervention, including motivational interviewing and function-based analysis procedures, as compared to a third usual care control group. A fourth group combining both interventions is also included in the study so as to examine its potential, relative effectiveness over either of the other two interventions alone.

The homeBase intervention typically includes up to six 60-minute sessions (i.e., home visits) and is designed to increase parental motivation and capacity to implement effective parenting practices. During homeBase, parents are encouraged to reflect upon their parenting practices and consider modifying those practices consistent with one or more of the five universal principles of positive behavior support that are central to the school module: (1) establish clear behavioral and performance expectations, (2) directly teach the expectations, (3) reinforce their display in schoolwork, (4) minimize teacher attention for minor inappropriate student behaviors, and (5) establish clear consequences for unacceptable behavior. In its current form, homeBase was constructed via an IES Goal 2 development grant 2008–2012; it was initially conceptualized as a revised home component to the First Step intervention. However, when the First Step Next intervention was redesigned without a true home intervention component, the team began to consider homeBase as a stand-alone intervention that could be valuable in isolation or in combination with any Tier II or Tier III school-based intervention that might benefit from the inclusion of parental support. This current study partially tests the viability of that assumption.

The relative contributions of these intervention components are being examined using a 2x2 factorial design in which K–3 students ($N = 400$) are randomly assigned to one of four study conditions: (a) First Step Next only, (b) homeBase only, (c) First Step Next plus homeBase, and (d) a usual-care, control condition. A multiple-gating approach is used to screen and identify eligible students with externalizing problem behaviors. Teachers randomized to school-only or school-plus-home intervention conditions receive training in the school component and ongoing, in-classroom support from a behavioral coach. Parents of children randomized to the home-only or school-plus-home intervention conditions are invited to participate in homeBase, completing up to six 60-minute home visitation sessions with a behavioral coach. The study examines the magnitude of immediate pre- and post-effects, the long-term maintenance of intervention effects, the mediators and moderators of student-level intervention effects, and implementation outcomes across school and home settings.

The team is particularly interested in characteristics of children who respond to each of the above interventions and in differential effects on a wide range of outcome measures. As in the preschool project, this study will include a diverse group of participants at sites in Kentucky and Indiana. Study participants are roughly equally divided across the four groups.

A comparative effectiveness study is an RCT designed to directly compare two different interventions in the same study. It also frequently compares the combined interventions to either one by itself (Alexander & Stafford, 2009). Preliminary results of both these projects are encouraging and, if successful, results of these studies should provide the fields of general and special education with evidence that First Step Next is reliably efficacious in reducing problem behaviors and increasing the prosocial behavior repertoires of at-risk students. In addition, they may also provide exploratory information on child and contextual factors that are important for implementation success.

## Future Planned Research on First Step Next

With regard to future research, the authors have long recognized the need for and importance of a universal component to complete the First Step intervention portfolio. A universal First Step intervention component would provide a seamless transition from Tier I to Tier II, allow for additional intervention-based screening to confirm the at-risk status of students who need more than simple exposure to a class-wide, universal intervention, and it would provide a foundation likely to enhance the overall efficacy of Tier II First Step Next. The major difference between a Tier I and Tier II First Step Next program version would be in the dosage received and the manner in which it is delivered. Thus, more students with challenging behavior could be served through a greater economy of scale within such a combined hybrid approach. It would likely also improve the program's adoption by end user consumers. Planning and design efforts are currently underway to produce a universal First Step Next component; the group will also be pursuing federal grants to support these efforts. Finally, the authors are in the early stages of developing and seeking federal funding for a large-scale, multisite dissemination research initiative for First Step Next in collaboration with SRI International Investigators.

## Conclusion

The First Step Program was long overdue for a major revision and update, given that nearly two decades had lapsed since its initial publication. This task involved a substantial investment of time and effort over a year-long period by a group of professionals with a diverse set of essential skills. The early results of this investment appear promising. However, the goals of making the First Step program more efficacious, streamlined and user friendly will ultimately be confirmed, or not, by current and future research outcomes and by more complete indications of end user adoption, acceptance and sustainability. With the addition of a "First Step for All" universal component, the authors expect that the added comprehensiveness and seamless transition between Tier I and Tier II levels of First Step Next will increase its appeal for program adopters and professional implementers. It is also to be hoped that the Tier III study will not only provide critical research data on the various components of First Step Next, but also pave the way for a more comprehensive and complete multi-tier system.

## Author note

The senior author wishes to acknowledge the myriad and invaluable contributions of three members of the First Step revision team: Marilyn Sprick and Cristy Coughlin of Pacific Northwest Publishing, Inc. and Brianna Stiller, the long-term First Step coordinator for the Eugene School District 4J. They brought critically important knowledge, skills and experiences to the revision process. Their dedicated efforts and extensive knowledge of instruction and best practices in applied interventions proved invaluable in reconstituting the original First Step program. In addition, Sara Ferris of Pacific Northwest Publishing served as a superb editor for all components of the revised program.

### References

Alexander, G. & Stafford, R. (2009). Does comparative effectiveness have a competitive edge? *Journal of the American Medical Association, 301*(23), 2488–2490.

Council for Children with Behavioral Disorders (2013). CCBD position summary on federal policy on disproportionality in special education. *Behavioral Disorders, 38*, 108–120.

DiPerna, J. (2006). Academic enablers and student achievement: Implications for assessment and intervention services in the schools. *Psychology in the Schools, 43*(1), 7–17.

Feil, E., Frey, A., Walker, H., Small, J., Seeley, J., Golly, A. & Forness, S. (2014). The efficacy of a home/school intervention for preschoolers with challenging behaviors: A randomized control trial of Preschool First Step to Success. *Journal of Early Intervention, 36*(3), 151–170.

Feil, E. G., Small, J., Seeley, J., Walker, H., Golly, A., Frey, A., & Forness, S. (2016). Early intervention for preschoolers at risk for attention-deficit/hyperactivity disorder. *Behavioral Disorders, 41*(2), 95–106.

Flay, B. R., Biglan, A., Boruch, R.F., Castro, F. G., Gottfredson, D., Kellam, S., Mościcki, E. K., Schinke, S., Valentine, J. C., Ji, P. (2005). Standards of evidence: criteria for efficacy, effectiveness and dissemination. *Prevention Science, 6*, 151–175.

Frey, A. J., Lee, J., Small, J., Seeley, J. R., Walker, H. M., & Feil, E. G. (2013). The Motivational Interviewing Guide: A process for enhancing teachers' motivation to adopt and implement school-based interventions. *Advances in School Mental Health Promotion.* doi:10.1080/1754730x.2013.804334

Frey, A., Small, J., Feil, E., Seeley, J., Walker, H., & Forness, S. (2015). First Step to Success: Applications to preschoolers at risk of developing Autism Spectrum Disorders. *Education and Training in Autism and Developmental Disabilities, 50*(4), 397–407.

Frey, A., Small, J., Feil, E., Seeley, J., Walker, H., & Golly, A. (2013). The feasibility of First Step to Success with preschoolers. *Students and Schools, 35*(3), 171–186.

Frey, A.J., Small, J.W., Lee, J., Walker, H.M., Seeley, J.R., Feil, E.G. & Golly, A. (2015). Expanding the range of the First Step to Success intervention: Tertiary-level support for teachers and families. *Early Childhood Research Quarterly, 30*, 1–11. doi:org/10.1016/j.ecresq.2014.05.002.

Menzies, W., Lane, K., & Lee, J. (2009). Self-monitoring strategies for use in the classroom: A promising support for productive behavior for students with emotional or behavioral disorders. *Beyond Behavior, 18*, 27–35.

Pennington, B. F. (2002). *The development of psychopathology.* New York, NY: Guilford.

Seeley, J., Small, J., Feil, E., Frey, A., Walker, H., Golly, A., & Forness, S. (in press). Effects of the First Step to Success early intervention on disruptive behavior and comorbid anxiety problems. *School Mental Health.*

Seeley, J., Small, J., Walker, H., Feil, E., Severson, H., Golly, A. & Forness, S. (2009). Efficacy of the First Step to Success intervention for students with attention deficit/hyperactivity disorder. *School Mental Health, 1*, 37–48.

Sumi, C., Woodbridge, M., Javitz, H., Thornton, P., Wagner, M., Rouspil, K., ... Severson, H. (2013) Assessing the effectiveness of First Step to Success: Are short-term results the first step to long-term behavioral improvements? *Journal of Emotional and Behavioral Disorders, 21*(1), 66–78.

Walker, H., Golly, A., McLane, J., & Kimmich, M. (2005). The Oregon First Step Replication Initiative: Statewide results of an evaluation of the program's impact. *Journal of Emotional and Behavioral Disorders, 13*(3), 163–172.

Walker, H., Kavanagh, K., Stiller, B., Golly, A., Feil, E. & Severson, H. (1997). *First Step to Success: Helping young children overcome antisocial behavior*. Longmont, CO: Sopris West, Inc.

Walker, H., Seeley, J., Small, J., Severson, H., Graham, B., Feil, E., ... Forness, S. (2009). A randomized controlled trial of the First Step to Success early intervention: Demonstration of program efficacy outcomes in a diverse, urban school district. *Journal of Emotional and Behavioral Disorders, 17*(4), 197–212.

Walker, H., Severson, H., Seeley, J., Feil, E., Small, J., Golly, A., ... Forness, S. (2014). The evidence base of the First Step to Success early intervention for preventing emerging antisocial behavior patterns. In H. Walker & F. Gresham (Eds.), *Handbook of evidence-based practices for emotional and behavioral disorders: Applications in schools*, (pp. 518–537). New York, NY: Guilford.

Walker, H., Stiller, B., Coughlin, C., Golly, A., Sprick, M., & Feil, E. (2015) *First Step Next*. Eugene, OR: Pacific Northwest Publishing, Inc.

Woodbridge, M., Sumi, C., Yu, J., Rouspil, K., Javitz, H., Seeley, J., & Walker, H. (2014). Implementation and sustainability of an evidence-based program: Lessons learned from the PRISM applied to First Step to Success. *Journal of Emotional and Behavioral Disorders, 22*(2), 95–106.

## Appendix A.
### *Super Student Skills Labels and Lesson Purpose*

| *Super Student Skill* | *Lesson Purpose* |
|---|---|
| **Do your best** | By reinforcing productive work behavior early, young students can obtain skills to support academic success in the future. This lesson teaches the student to work quietly and put forth his/her best effort at school. |
| **Be cool** | Many young students need to learn how to de-escalate before frustration turns into a disruptive temper tantrum. This lesson teaches the focus student to recognize feelings of frustration and use a three-step procedure for positively coping with these feelings. |
| **Mistakes are okay** | Mistakes are often a trigger for disruptive behaviors. The steps introduced in this lesson help a student diffuse frustration. Because mistakes are essential for learning, this skill provides a gateway to both behavioral and academic learning. |
| **Be safe** | Knowing the difference between safe and unsafe behavior is a critical skill that every young child must learn. This lesson teaches the focus student three basic rules that set the foundation for safe behavior at school. |
| **Follow directions** | Learning to follow directions is a basic behavioral skill. The skill of following directions operationalizes being cooperative. By learning how to follow directions, the young First Step NEXT student gains the means to achieve school success. |
| **Ask for attention the right way** | Some students have difficulty adjusting to the school context where adult attention must be shared among a group of children. By providing the focus student with an explicit signal to solicit help from a teacher, this lesson teaches the student to ask for adult attention in a way that minimizes disruption to the class. |
| **Be a team player** | The school setting often requires students to participate as part of a group. This lesson frames this group as a team, and the focus student is taught basic skills for how to be a good team player when working with classmates, including how to use kind, polite, and helpful words when interacting with others. |

# Teaming with Families of Young Children with Autism Spectrum Disorder to Prevent Challenging Behavior

*Tia R. Schultz, Suzanne Kucharczyk, Melissa A. Sreckovic, and Angel Fettig*

## Abstract

A young child's challenging behavior can greatly disrupt family routines, activities, and interactions. Such disruptions can be especially difficult for families with children with autism spectrum disorder (ASD) who report significant levels of stress as a group. Children with ASD, given characteristic difficulties with communication and restrictive behaviors, can exhibit challenging behavior in lieu of communicative behavior that may not be in their repertoire. Recently, reviews of research on interventions used with young children with ASD in applied settings such as school, home, and community have identified practices effective in preventing challenging behavior. This paper describes such evidence-based practices, suggests ways in which these can be applied in the home, and provides strategies for teaching and coaching families on implementation of strategies.

Keywords: parent-implemented, autism spectrum disorder (ASD), evidence-based practices, behavior support, coaching, prevention, challenging behavior, parent-professional collaboration

## Introduction

Autism spectrum disorder (ASD) is a neurodevelopmental disorder involving challenges in social communication and interaction with the presence of narrow, restricted behaviors, interests, or activities (American Psychiatric Association [APA], 2013). All individuals with ASD demonstrate some level of concern across these domains;

however, the symptoms are expressed in a variety of ways and the severity of impairment varies from person to person (Phetrasuwan, Miles, & Mesibov, 2009). While challenging behavior is not a defining feature of ASD, because of delays in communication, language, and social development, challenging behaviors are commonly observed in individuals with ASD throughout their life span (Matson & Nebel-Schwalm, 2007). Challenging behaviors may be present in myriad ways among young children with ASD, including physical aggression, property destruction, tantrums, defiance, and self-injury (Brereton, Tonge, & Einfeld, 2006; Horner, Carr, Strain, Todd, & Reed, 2002). These undesirable behaviors serve a communicative function (Horner et al., 2002), and it often takes less effort for a child with ASD to engage in the challenging behavior than to attempt verbal communication to achieve a desired outcome.

Young children's challenging behaviors can negatively impact academic outcomes, peer relationships, and family quality of life and experiences (Dunlap et al., 2006a). Studies have shown that emotional and behavioral problems of young children with ASD have been associated with parental mental health and stress (e.g, Herring, Gray, Taffe, Sweeny, & Einfield, 2006). Family routines and participation in desired activities can also be impacted by children with ASD due to their experiences with their environments. Families have noted the intense preparation involved in attending an activity, including developing alternative plans and exit strategies, as well as avoiding specific activities that have been or could be prob-lematic for the child (Bagby, Dickie, & Baranek, 2012). Prevention and intervention efforts to address children's challenging behavior is critical; without supports in place these behaviors are likely to persist or worsen over time (Horner et al., 2002).

Evidence-based social-emotional frameworks for children (e.g., Pyramid Model; Powell, Dunlap, & Fox, 2006) have highlighted positive social-emotional development as essential in preventing challenging behaviors in young children. At the foundation of prevention is the formation of positive relationships with adults (e.g., parents, caregivers, teachers; Powell et al., 2006). These positive relationships help support social-emotional growth and can eventually lead to positive relationships with peers. It is also essential that families and caregivers establish clear, consistent routines and expectations that promote positive interactions. Further, families and caregivers teach children social-emotional skills, such as expressing and regulating emotions and demonstrating empathy. For young children with ASD, these are the most difficult skills to develop because of struggles with social interaction and communication (APA, 2013). Therefore, families and practitioners will likely need to systematically implement evidence-based interventions to prevent children's challenging behavior and promote healthy social-emotional development. The foundation of prevention of young children's challenging behavior is focused in the home and in the relationship between the child and caregivers, making it imperative that prevention and intervention efforts take a family-centered approach.

## Family Centered Approach to Implementation

Challenging behaviors are among the most significant challenges faced by families of young children with ASD (Herring et al., 2006); therefore, supporting parents in using evidence-based practices to address these behaviors in home settings is crucial. Family is the most central and constant resource in young children's development as family members serve as the "shapers" of children's learning and behavior starting at birth. Involving parents, caregivers, and other family members in preventing and addressing young children's challenging behaviors is more powerful than providing intervention exclusively to the child (Dawson et al., 2010; Friedman, Woods, & Salisbury, 2012; McWilliam, 2010). Many studies have demonstrated that family members can successfully assume the role of interventionist in addressing challenging behaviors with the right support from professionals (e.g., Fettig & Barton, 2014; Fettig, Schultz, & Sreckovic, 2015; Lucyshyn et al., 2007).

In 2017, the Division for Early Childhood (DEC) revised their position statement on challenging behaviors and re-emphasized the important role families play in designing and implementing interventions to address challenging behavior (2017). A child's family spends the most time with the child and is the constant in the child's life. As young children develop within the context of relationships (Shonkoff & Phillips, 2000), understanding and valuing the role of caregiving relationships is necessary to support children's social and emotional development. Several principles of working with families are critical to consider as professionals treat family members as integral partners in addressing children's challenging behaviors and social-emotional needs. These include: (a) valuing and respecting family philosophy, cultures, and goals; (b) sharing information with families; (c) being flexible and responsive to families' needs and choices; and (d) involving families in designing interventions and supports (DEC, 2017). It is only when these principles are implemented that parents and caregivers perceive themselves as key participating members of the intervention team. Professionals must create a process in which all team members respect the unique values and priorities of families, promote family strengths, and support a family's sense of confidence and competence (Dunst, 2001; Keilty, 2010). This will foster positive outcomes for children.

In this family-centered approach, professionals serve as coaches and supports, ensuring that families and caregivers are equipped with evidence-based practices (EBP) to address behaviors and that they have the resources to implement these practices in natural environments. Fidelity of parent interventions is highly associated with the implementation supports families receive in authentic settings (Fixsen, Naoom, Blasé, Friedman, & Wallace, 2005; O'Donnell, 2008). When interventions move from didactic training to natural implementation settings, the fidelity of implementation can be negatively impacted if appropriate supports are not provided to families (Dickinson, 2011; Marulis & Neuman, 2010). Therefore, coaching and training supports parents receive to effectively implement evidence-based strategies in natural contexts are crucial for yielding positive child outcomes (Powell & Dunlap, 2010; Fettig & Barton, 2014).

Given the critical need in supporting families of children with ASD to address challenging behaviors, this paper aims to provide interdisciplinary professionals with strategies for working with families of young children with ASD to implement EBP to prevent, reduce, and eliminate challenging behavior. This paper considers how a family-first philosophy, knowledge of focused interventions found to be effective with children with ASD, and emerging family coaching and teaming practices can be merged in order to support families. First, EBP for preventing the challenging behavior of young children with ASD are described, along with examples of families implementing the interventions. Second, this paper provides a description and illustration of the coaching process that can be used to support families in their implementation of EBP.

## Evidence-Based Practices for Preventing Behavioral Challenges

In 2015, The National Professional Development Center (NPDC) for ASD conducted a comprehensive review of research on all focused interventions with children with ASD from birth to 22 years of age (Wong et al., 2015). Twenty-seven EBP were identified across skill domains; of these, 21 have been shown to be effective in addressing challenging behavior for individuals 0–5 and/or 6–14 years of age. These practices provide practitioners and families with research-based strategies to prevent, reduce, and eliminate challenging behavior of children with ASD. The following strategies are highlighted because research has documented their effectiveness to support prevention or reduction of challenging behavior in natural settings (e.g., school, home, community), and they are foundational practices in that they are often used in conjunction with other EBP. Importantly, they can be implemented fairly easily by parents because they require little training and few resources.

Each strategy is described below, including an example of what each may look like when implemented with families (see Table 1).

## Antecedent-based Intervention (ABI)

In ABI, variables that trigger a challenging behavior are identified in order to make changes that will prevent the challenging behavior from occurring and promote replacement skills instead (Sam & AFIRM Team, 2016). A functional behavior assessment (FBA) may be conducted by a trained professional to identify these key variables (e.g., demands placed, desired object unavailable). Parent implementation of ABI focuses on preventing future occurrences of challenging behavior by creating an environment that reduces the need for the child to use challenging behaviors (e.g., changing the physical environment to ensure success, provide access to communication, modify routine or schedule, create more structure, increase interest, provide choices) and promotes the use of replacement behaviors (Neitzel, 2010). ABI can be used to decrease the following behaviors: challenging behavior, aggression, self-injurious behavior, and stereotypic behavior (Sam & AFIRM Team, 2016).

*The Valdeen family was concerned because their daughter struggled with transitioning from home to community outings. When it was time to leave the house, she screamed and threw items around the room. The family worked with their daughter's team, and decided to implement some ABI strategies. First, ten minutes before they were ready to leave, the family set a timer and gave their daughter a verbal cue that they would be leaving in ten minutes. Then they presented her with a visual schedule of what to expect on the outing. They also let her choose between two comfort objects to bring along with her. When it was time to leave, they brought the visual schedule and the comfort items along to the car. These modifications (e.g., use of timer, visual schedule, comfort objects) provided their daughter with the cues and supports she needed to manage transitions.*

## Differential Reinforcement (Reinforcement and Extinction)

Reinforcement is a consequence that increases the likelihood that a behavior will continue in the future, and extinction is the absence of reinforcement following a behavior. Combining these two strategies is differential reinforcement, which is a powerful combination of strategies that leads to positive outcomes for young children (Savage & AFIRM Team, 2017). If a child uses challenging behavior to gain attention, differential reinforcement would include praise of appropriate behavior while ignoring challenging behavior. Differential reinforcement can decrease off-task behavior, non-compliance, and destructive or aggressive behavior (Vismara, Bogin, & Sullivan, 2010).

*The Rodriguez family realized that when their son had tantrums at mealtime (e.g., lying on the floor yelling and kicking), he received quite a bit of attention from adults (e.g., pleas to stop, frustrated sighs, bribes when in public). Instead of providing attention (i.e., reinforcement), the family gave him attention when he was engaging in appropriate tasks and ignored the tantrum behavior. During the next mealtime, the family talked with their child as he ate his meal and praised him for completing his meal tasks (e.g., wiping his spot, scooping his food). When he started to whine or yell, the family ignored that behavior. Once he returned to displaying appropriate behavior, such as eating, they continued their positive interactions with him.*

## Prompting and Time Delay

Prompting is a strategy that gives the child cues after the initial directive, but before the child responds. The prompt is intended to increase the likelihood the child will respond to the directive successfully (Sam & AFIRM Team, 2015a). Prompting can be used by itself, but is more effective when paired with time delay, which is a procedure to fade prompts (Sam & AFIRM Team, 2015b). Types of prompting cues include gestures, verbal, visual, physical, and modeling (Neitzel & Wolery, 2010). All of these types of prompts can be faded with time delay procedures.

*The Jackson family found that their son would throw blocks and yell during playtime when he could not get his blocks to stay stacked in a tower. They decided to use prompting to help him be more successful with building. During play, they sat with him while he built towers. In the beginning, they immediately pointed to which blocks to use and where to stack them in order of size. Once he was successful, the family used time delay to fade out their gestural prompts by giving their child three seconds to independently choose and place the block before using the prompt. They were careful to immediately praise his independence specifically (e.g., "Great! The small block goes on the big block!") If within 3 seconds, their son showed frustration (e.g., yelling, crying, beginning to throw blocks) his parents immediately provided gestures and physical prompts and reinforced him for being successful.*

## Naturalistic Intervention

Naturalistic intervention uses principles of applied behavior analysis in natural settings and routines to help children learn skills (Amsbary & AFIRM Team, 2017). Naturalistic intervention includes using novel items during tasks and play, responding to what the child is saying, imitating what the child is saying or doing, expanding on what the child is saying, giving choices to the child, and following the child's lead (Amsbary & AFIRM Team, 2017). Naturalistic intervention has been shown to increase social-communication skills, specifically spontaneous language; requesting; increased complexity, amount, and diversity in language; increased social interactions; joint attention; and decreased disruptive behavior (Amsbary & AFIRM Team, 2017).

*The Amari family wanted to help their son build his communication skills. They believed it would also help reduce how often he yelled and screamed if he could more effectively communicate his wants and needs. They implemented naturalistic intervention by targeting his communication skills during typical family routines. Throughout the day, they expanded on what their child was saying and gave choices. For example, during bath time, they asked their child if he wanted to take the boat or truck in the bath. When he pointed to the boat, they said, "You chose the boat." When he said, "Boat!" they replied, "You have the blue boat!" They did the same with any attempts he made at using words to request items. As his language skills increased, he was able to verbalize his needs, and decreased the need to scream or yell.*

## Visual Supports

Visual supports are concrete prompts or pre-signals that let children know what they should be or will be doing (Sam & AFIRM Team, 2015c). They can be used alone or paired with verbal cues. Visual supports fall into three categories: boundaries, schedules, and cues (Sam & AFIRM Team, 2015c). Boundary visual supports involve arranging the room to increase on-task behavior. Schedules depict the order in which activities/tasks are going to happen, which increases children's understanding of what is expected and can help them transition between activities. Visual cues can be used to show children where items are, which options are available to them, and/or how to complete a task, which can help with independence. Visual supports can also help children decrease challenging behavior related to task completion, and adjust to changes (Smith, 2008).

*The Johnson family's 6 year old daughter was distractible during the morning routine. Despite being capable of completing each morning task in the routine, she rarely completed any of the tasks without constant verbal prompts, and sometimes other family members completed tasks for her. The high level of verbal prompting made her irritable and the Johnson family was often late for school and work. The Johnson family decided to post a visual schedule in the kitchen for the morning routine. Each day, they would take their daughter to the schedule to review the morning tasks. The schedule included pictures of their daughter engaging in the following tasks: eating breakfast, brushing teeth, putting on shoes. As she completed a task, she would cross it off the list with a dry erase marker.*

## Video Modeling

Video modeling involves a video-recorded example of the individual or another person performing the target task, which the individual views before performing the task (LaCava, 2013). There are three types of video modeling: self-modeling, point-of-view modeling, and video prompting (LaCava, 2013). Video self-modeling is a recording of the individual successfully performing the task. Point-of-view modeling is a recording of what the task looks like through the eyes of the individual. Video prompting shows the task in steps with pauses after each step, giving the individual an opportunity to complete that portion of the task. Video modeling is only considered an evidence-based intervention for children ages 6 to 14 years of age (not children 3 to 5) (Wong, et al., 2015).

*The Yin family was concerned because their daughter would not brush her teeth. To help her, they created a video of their daughter brushing her teeth. They prompted her through each step, then edited out the prompts, so the video showed her brushing her teeth independently. In the evening, they showed her the video before she brushed her teeth.*

These evidence-based practices can be implemented in home, community, and school settings to reduce the challenging behaviors of young children. However, identifying the appropriate practice is just the first step. It is imperative the practice be implemented with fidelity, across environments to promote generalization of skills, and with key stakeholders. Research consistently demonstrates the benefits of implementing interventions with young children over time, in multiple environments, and with families as key contributors (Dunlap, Ester, Langhans, & Fox, 2006b).

## Coaching Families through Implementation of EBP

Building family capacity to effectively implement evidence-based strategies from a foundation of family-centered philosophy and practices can greatly affect the outcomes of young children with ASD. As early intervention service models shift from child-directed services to a focus on the parent-child relationship and interaction (Campbell & Sawyer, 2009; Friedman et al., 2012; McWilliam, 2010) opportunities emerge to prepare parents to implement evidence-based practices. Aligned with this shift, research on the implementation of EBP for young children with disabilities has been increasingly studied in applied settings, such as in the home, with the parent as primary interventionist. For example, studies have demonstrated that parents can collaborate with professionals to assess and effectively address their child's challenging behaviors that interfere with family activities and interactions (Fettig et al., 2015, Lucyshyn et al., 2007). Further, studies of parent implementation have focused on children with ASD and the use of behavioral practices such as those discussed previously (Barton & Fettig, 2013; Hong et al., 2016). As intervention implementation shifts to parents, interventionists take on the responsibility of coaching parents through a systematic and cyclical process of support through planning, observing, modeling, reflecting, and provision of feedback.

Preparing parents to implement EBP has taken multiple approaches across two categories: traditional (e.g., in person training, coaching) and non-traditional (e.g., telehealth or telepractice coaching, online instruction). Traditional methods include face-to-face didactic training, in-the-moment performance feedback, and coaching. Rush and Sheldon (2011) identify five characteristics of family coaching: joint planning, observations, action, reflection, and feedback. In collaboration with Rush and Sheldon, Kucharczyk et al. (2012) merged the NPDC on ASD's coaching model with the resources for parent implementation designed by the Family, Infant and Preschool Program (FIPP) Center for the Advanced Study of Excellence (CASE) in Early Childhood and Family Support Practices (2017). The following section describes this coaching process.

## Family-Centered Coaching Process

Aligned with this model, practitioners coaching families use an iterative process grounded in family-centered practices, adult learning practices, and led by family priorities. Coaching is a sequential and systematic process that is mutual, in that family and interventions make decisions about how coaching unfolds through information gathering, goal setting and scaling, joint planning, observations and actions between parents and interventionists, reflection on implementation, and ongoing feedback. The following example describes each of these steps of the coaching process for a family preparing to implement EBP to support their child's behavior.

*The Crouch family is struggling with their son's challenging behavior during transitions between activities at home. Their son cries, screams, and falls to the floor at the beginning of transitions such as coming to the breakfast table after getting dressed, getting ready to leave for an errand with his parents, stopping solitary play with toys to get ready for bed, and so on. The behavior has become so disruptive that his family has minimized the amount of transitions in order to cope, but this has had an impact on their interactions together and activities outside the home.*

*The interventionist and Crouch family begin by <u>gathering information</u> about family routines and priorities specific to the challenging behavior and that would impact their implementation of EBP. The family identifies negotiable and non-negotiable routines or activities, activities that are more or less preferred by their son, and considers aspects of the EBP that may be challenging to implement. Together, the family and interventionist complete reinforcement questionnaires to identify ways in which their son would prefer to be reinforced. After information is gathered on their son's behavior and family routines,* *priorities and goals are developed. During this phase, observable and measurable goals are developed specific to changes they would like to see in their child's behavior (e.g., an increase in adaptive behavior, a decrease in challenging behavior). They also develop goals specific to their own behavior. Goals are scaled (Ruble, Mcgrew, & Toland, 2012) to identify incremental steps towards the ultimate goal.*

*Once the child's goals and preferences, as well as the family's routines and activities are clear, the family and interventionist consider appropriate EBP. After reviewing appropriate EBP, the Crouch family decide to prepare to implement differential reinforcement (e.g., reinforcing behavior during transitions that is not crying, screaming, and falling to the floor), antecedent-based interventions (e.g., ensuring that less preferred activities are followed by preferred activities), and visual supports (e.g., a "first/then" visual to alert their son that a preferred activity will occur after the transition or less preferred activity). Once these EBP are identified the interventionist and family make a plan for coaching which includes goals for the family's use of these EBP (e.g., consistent use of EBP as planned).*

*This preparatory work of coaching is essential to ensure a strong foundation built on understanding of the family, their daily lives, strengths, and priority needs. Next, the interventionist and family engage in a cyclical process of pre-observation, observation and action, and post-observation reflection and feedback. During pre-observations, which may occur formally at the beginning of each session together or informally through phone calls, e-mails, and texts, the coach checks in on the family's use of the EBP, provides instruction if needed, and makes a plan for observation and action. Conscious co-planning coaching ensures that the relationship between family and interventionist remains grounded in mutual trust and respect.*

*Pre-observations are followed by observations and actions. Observations and actions, as described by Kucharczyk et al. (2012), include the interventionist's modeling of the use of EBP for a parent or observations of implementation by parents or other caregivers which may include in-the-moment feedback as decided by the Crouch family and interventionist. After observations and modeling actions, the interventionist, as coach, engages the Crouch family in reflection on their child's progress, as well as on their implementation, in order to help identify concerns, consider next steps, and uncover any need for additional support. In addition to reflection, the coach provides feedback on the family's implementation based on data collected and seeks feedback on their own coaching behaviors from the family.*

As illustrated in the Crouch family example, coaching as described by the NPDC on ASD (Kucharczyk et al., 2012) is a systematic, sequential process grounded in trust and mutual respect between family and practitioner. The coaching process includes information gathering, goal setting and scaling, identification of EBP, joint planning, pre-observation check-ins, observations and actions, and post-observation feedback and reflection.

## Coaching Adaptations

A variant on face-to-face coaching is covert coaching, which allows the coach to communicate with the parent from a different location (e.g., from another room), thus minimizing the negative effects of their presence on the parent-child interaction. Covert coaching has been effective when used by co-teachers through peer coaching (Scheeler, Cogdon, & Stansbery, 2010); with pre-service professionals (Artman-Meeker, Rosenber, Badgett, Yang, & Penney, 2017; Scheeler, Bruno, Grubb, & Seavey, 2009); and when provided to young adults and adolescents with ASD and other disabilities (Bennett, Ramasamy, & Honsberger, 2013). Covert audio coaching can also be used to support families in implementing EBP (Oliver & Brady, 2014). Covert audio coaching is provided through a wireless device (e.g., an ear bud) with coaches providing prompting and feedback away from the caregiver/child pair. Using covert coaching could be incorporated in the coaching process described during the observation and action phase. For example, using covert coaching, the interventionist could observe the parent working with their child over a platform such as Skype while providing feedback over a wireless headset.

## Online Learning Supports for Coaching

With the omnipresence of the internet and access to smartphones, tablets, laptops and other devices, online instruction has become a popular mode by which to disseminate knowledge to professionals and parents. Platforms such as Autism Focused Intervention Resources and Modules (AFIRM, 2015) and Autism Internet Modules (AIM, n.d.) provide online instruction on the implementation of EBP for children with ASD through text, video, links to resources, and implementation checklists. Other websites directly target parents with information on the implementation of EBP for children and youth with ASD. Examples are the ASD Toddler Initiative (n.d.) and the Autism Distance Education Parent Training (ADEPT, 2017). Online instruction provides opportunities to access knowledge without the additional burden of travel and time costs associated with attending training sessions. Incorporating online instruction during joint planning and reflection phases of coaching can ensure that parents and practitioners use the same language, reflect on similar examples of implementation, and have access to the same implementation checklists and other resources.

## Coaching at a Distance

In addition to online training, technology has facilitated parent learning of EBP and implementation through the use of telehealth or telepractice. These methods are modeled on telemedicine technologies which link geographically isolated patients with medical professionals (American Telemedicine Association, 2013). Frequently, telehealth models incorporate a hybrid of online training and coaching using platforms such as Skype (Meadan et al., 2016); or an intervention-specific online learning platform (e.g., Wainer & Ingersoll, 2013; 2015); or video-conferencing platforms (Heitzman-

Powell, Buzhardt, Rusinko, & Miller, 2014). Heitzman-Powell et al. (2014) described a program for teaching parents of children with ASD to implement EBP by merging online learning modules and telepractice coaching. After completion of the learning module, families received coaching using video-conferencing at a local telemedicine site closer to their home. Heitzman-Powell et al. (2014) reported that four families who participated in a module on the use of applied behavior analysis saved themselves 9,052 miles of driving by using this hybrid of online instruction and telehealth intervention.

Face-to face-reflection, monitoring of those involved in implementing, and monitoring the child's progress demand that all practitioners working with a family are working toward the same family-centered goals. It is important to recognize the stress and work it can add for families to have multiple professionals in their lives. Below are some considerations for partnering effectively with families.

## Considerations

As has been stated, families play an important role in preventing and intervening on children's challenging behaviors. Involving families in the service delivery for infants and toddlers with disabilities is also mandated under Part C of the Individuals with Disabilities Education Improvement Act (IDEIA, 2004). Interdisciplinary and transdisciplinary (Boyer & Thompson 2014; King et al., 2009) models have been described within early childhood settings as processes for effective collaboration within complex systems. It is crucial that professionals working with young children within early intervention or school settings must collaborate with families and caretakers to ensure that they are equipped with EBP to effectively address their young children's challenging behaviors. This comprehensive interdisciplinary team should also include healthcare professionals who provide much of the needed support on issues around sleeping, toileting, and other healthcare needs.

Working in interdisciplinary teams can support families in home, clinic, and school settings in implementing evidence-based practices. Professionals (e.g., speech language pathologists, occupational therapists, behavior specialists, healthcare providers) often work on similar goals and skills for the same child they work with. When the team is consistent in how they address a challenging behavior, the challenges will likely decrease more quickly (Donaldson, Stahmer, Nippold, & Camarata, 2014). Further, each team member may have a unique perspective on the child's progress. Sharing observations and methods of data collection can provide a better picture of the child's progress (Donaldson et al., 2014).

The importance of cultural considerations when addressing the challenging behavior of young children cannot be underestimated. When working with families, it is critical to recognize that families are diverse in a variety of domains, including family structure and ability levels, race and ethnicity, spoken languages, and socioeconomic structure (Friesen, Hanson, & Martin, 2015), all of which can impact child behavior and family expectations, priorities, and goals. Families and practitioners may view the child's behavior through two different lenses, further emphasizing the importance of family and practitioner collaboration. Even families and practitioners from the same cultural or ethnic group may have different beliefs and values (Friesen et al., 2015). Therefore, practitioners should engage in continuous reflection to recognize how their own personal values, preconceptions, and biases may affect their perception of a child's behavior and how that may differ from the families with whom they work (DEC 2017; Friesen et al., 2015;). Further, practitioners are encouraged to seek input from families regarding their values, expectations, priorities, and goals for their child, as well as, information on the family's beliefs related to childrearing and discipline (Friesen et al., 2015). Practitioners can glean this information through interviewing the family, asking the family to share stories, visiting the child's home and asking the family to walk through a typical day, and learning about other cultural perspectives (Friesen et al.,

2015; Lynch, 2011). Family diversity will impact the behavioral goals for the child and prevention and intervention supports. Therefore, working collaboratively with families to understand their philosophy and design prevention and intervention supports to address children's challenging behavior is key.

## Conclusion

Families of young children with ASD who engage in persistent challenging behaviors face considerable demands that impact their daily routines and ability to participate in community activities. With support in implementing EBP, families can effectively prevent and address challenging behaviors and improve their overall quality of life. Enhancing family capacity to address these behaviors is crucial. Professionals must serve as the support agents to strengthen parent-child relationships and enhance families' competence and confidence to address their child's challenging behaviors and promote their child's development.

## Table 1.
### Foundational EBP to Prevent and Reduce Challenging Behavior of Young Children with ASD

| EBP | Definition | Considerations for choosing this EBP | Tips for supporting families |
|---|---|---|---|
| **ABI** | Rearranging environment, routines, and activities to prevent challenging behavior | Combine ABI with reinforcement of appropriate behavior | Embed across family routines |
| **Differential reinforcement (reinforcement/ extinction)** | Providing positive and desired consequences for target behaviors or behaviors other than those that are challenging | Reinforcement: change reinforcers periodically so child does not get bored Extinction: expect a short period of the challenging behavior getting worse before it gets better | Use items already in the family home or activities the family already uses as reinforcement |
| **Time delay/ prompting** | Systematically delaying prompts to increase the likelihood the desired behavior occurs independently | Delaying prompts can be difficult; practicing wait time is important | Help family members develop a system to delay prompts (e.g., counting to self, distractions) |
| **Naturalistic intervention** | Using strategies in naturally-occurring settings and activities to promote learning and communication | Parents may need help to delay their inclination to help rather than create natural opportunities to promote communication | Embed across family routines |
| **Visual supports** | Using visual displays (e.g., schedule, visual boundaries, organization systems) to promote use of target behaviors and increase independence | Determine ahead of time, which type of visual supports are most helpful for the child (e.g., pictures, words); use visual supports that are understood by the child (e.g., photographs, line drawings, real objects) | If using pictures, create with photos taken in the family's home; if using words, use the family's preferred language |
| **Video models** | Using video examples to demonstrate successful completion of tasks as a tool for teaching skills | Ensure that necessary technology is easily accessible to parents and will not stress family resources; capitalize on family skills in choosing technology | Work with families to meet their technology needs (professional makes videos vs. family makes videos) |

## References

AFIRM Team (2015). Autism Focused Intervention Resources and Modules (AFIRM). Chapel Hill, NC: National Professional Development Center on Autism Spectrum Disorder, FPG Child Development Center, University of North Carolina. Retrieved from http://afirm.fpg.unc.edu/

American Psychiatric Association (2013). *Diagnostic and statistical manual of mental disorders* (5th Ed.). Arlington, VA: American Psychiatric Association.

American Telemedicine Association (2013). Telemedicine defined. Retrieved from http://www.americantelemed.org/ i4a/pages/index.cfm?pageid=3333

Amsbary, J., & AFIRM Team (2017). *Naturalistic intervention*. Chapel Hill, NC: National Professional Development Center on Autism Spectrum Disorder, FPG Child Development Center, University of North Carolina. Retrieved from http://afirm.fpg.unc.edu/Naturalistic-intervention

Artman-Meeker, K., Rosenberg, N., Badgett, N., Yang, X., & Penney, A. (2017). The effects of bug-in ear coaching on pre-service behavior analysts' use of functional communication training. *Behavior Analysis in Practice, 10*(3), 228–241.

*Autism Internet Modules* (AIM) (n.d.) Ohio Center for Autism and Low Incidence (OCALI). Retrieved from http://www.autisminternetmodules.org/

Autism Distance Education Parent Training (ADEPT). (2017). Sacramento, CA: UC Davis Mind Institute. Retrieved from http://ucdmc.ucdavis.edu/mindinstitute/centers/cedd/cedd_adept.html

Autism Spectrum Disorders (ASD) Toddler Initiative (n.d.) Chapel Hill, NC: National Professional Development Center on Autism Spectrum Disorder, FPG Child Development Center, University of North Carolina. Retrieved from http://asd-toddler.fpg.unc.edu/

Bagby, M. S., Dickie, V. A., & Baranek, G. T. (2012). How sensory experiences of children with and without autism affect family occupations. *The American Journal of Occupational Therapy, 66*(1), 78–86.

Barton, E. E., & Fettig, A. (2013). Parent-implemented interventions for young children with disabilities. *Journal of Early Intervention, 35*(2), 194–219.

Bennett, K. D., Ramasamy, R., & Honsberger, T. (2013). Further examination of covert audio coaching on improving employment skills among secondary students with autism. *Journal of Behavioral Education, 22*, 103–119.

Boyer, V. E., & Thompson, S. D. (2014). Transdisciplinary model and early intervention: Building collaborative relationships. *Young Exceptional Children, 17*(3), 19–32.

Brereton, A. V., Tonge, B. J., & Einfeld, S. L. (2006). Psychopathology in children and adolescents with autism compared to young people with intellectual disability. *Journal of Autism and Developmental Disorders, 36*(7), 863–70.

Campbell, P. H. & Sawyer, L. B. (2009). Changing early intervention providers' home visiting skills through participation in professional development. *Topics in Early Childhood Special Education, 28*, 219–234.

Dawson, G., Rogers, S., Munson, J., Smith, M., Winter, J., Greenson, J., .... Varley, J. (2010).Randomized, controlled trial of an intervention for toddlers with autism: The Early Start. Denver Model. *Pediatrics, 125*(1), e17–e23.

Dickinson, D. K. (2011). Teachers' language practices and academic outcomes of preschool children. *Science, 333*(6045), 964–967.

Division for Early Childhood. (2017). *Position Statement on Challenging Behavior and Young Children*. Washington D.C.: Author.

Donaldson, A. A., Stahmer, A. C., Nippold, M. & Camarata, S. (2014). Team collaboration: The use of behavior principles for serving students with ASD. *Language, Speech & Hearing Services in Schools, 45*(4), 261–276.

Dunlap, G., Strain, P. S., Fox, L., Carta, J. J., Conroy, M., Smith, B. J., ... Sowell, C. (2006a). Prevention and intervention with young children's challenging behavior: Perspectives regarding current knowledge. *Behavioral Disorders, 32*(1), 29–45.

Dunlap, G., Ester, T., Langhans, S., & Fox, L. (2006b). Functional communication training with toddlers in home environments. *Journal of Early Intervention, 28*, 81–96.

Dunst, C. J. (2001). Participation of young children with disabilities in community learning activities. In M. Guralnick (ed.), *Early childhood inclusion: Focus on change* (pp. 307–333). Baltimore, MD: Paul H. Brookes Publishing Co.

Family, Infant and Preschool Program (FIPP) Center for the Advanced Study of Excellence (CASE) in *Early Childhood and Family Support Practices*. (2017). Retrieved from http://fipp.org

Fettig, A., & Barton, E. E. (2014). Parent implementation of function-based intervention to reduce children's challenging behavior: A literature review. *Topics in Early Childhood Special Education, 34*(1), 49–61.

Fettig, A., Schultz, T. R., & Sreckovic, M. A. (2015). Effects of coaching on the implementation of functional assessment–based parent intervention in reducing challenging behaviors. *Journal of Positive Behavior Interventions, 17*(3), 170–180.

Fixsen, D. L., Naoom, S. F., Blasé, K. A., Friedman, R. M., & Wallace, F. (2005). *Implementation research: A synthesis of the literature* (FMHI Publication No. 231). Tampa, FL: University of South Florida, Louis de la Parte Florida Mental Health Institute, National Implementation Research Network.

Friedman, M., Woods, J., & Salisbury, C. (2012). Caregiver coaching strategies for early intervention providers: Moving toward operational definitions. *Infants & Young Children, 25*(1), 62–82.

Friesen, A., Hanson, M., & Martin, K. (2015). In the eyes of the beholder: Cultural considerations in interpreting children's behaviors. *Young Exceptional Children, 18*(4), 19–30.

Heitzman-Powell, L. S., Buzhardt, J., Rusinko, L. C., & Miller, T. M. (2014). Formative evaluation of an ABA outreach training program for parents of children with autism in remote areas. *Focus on Autism and Other Developmental Disabilities, 29*(1), 23–38.

Herring, S., Gray, J., Taffe, B., Sweeny, D., & Einfeld, S. (2006). Behaviour and emotional problems in toddlers with pervasive developmental disorders and developmental delay: Associations with parental mental health and family functioning. *Journal of Intellectual Disability Research, 50*, 874–882.

Hong, E. R., Ganz, J. B., Neely, L., Boles, M., Gerow, S., & Davis, J. L. (2016). A meta-analytic review of family-implemented social and communication interventions for individuals with developmental disabilities. Review. *Journal of Autism and Developmental Disorders, 3*(2), 125–136.

Horner, R., Carr, E. G., Strain, P. S., Todd, A. W., & Reed, H. K. (2002). Problem behavior interventions for young children with autism: A research synthesis. *Journal of Autism and Developmental Disorders, 32*(5), 423–446.

Individuals with Disabilities Education Improvement Act of 2004, P.L. 108–446, 20 U.S.C. § 1400 *et seq.*

Keilty, B. (2010). *The early intervention guidebook for families and professionals: Partnering for success.* New York, NY: Teachers College Press.

King, G., Strachan, D., Tucker, M., Duwyn, B., Desserud, S., & Shillington, M. (2009). The application of a transdisciplinary model for early intervention services. *Infants & Young Children, 22*(3), 211–223.

Kucharczyk, S., Shaw. E., Smith Myles, B., Sullivan, L., Szidon, K., & Tuchman-Ginsberg, L. (2012). *Guidance & coaching on evidence-based practices for learners with autism spectrum disorders.* Chapel Hill: The University of North Carolina, Frank Porter Graham Child Development Institute, National Professional Development Center on Autism Spectrum Disorders.

LaCava, P. (2013). Video modeling: An online training module. (Kansas City: University of Kansas, Special Education Department). In Ohio Center of Autism and Low Incidence (OCALI), *Autism Internet Modules*, www.autismint-ernetmodules.org. Columbus, OH: OCALI.

Lucyshyn, J. M., Albin, R. W., Horner, R. H., Mann, J. C., Mann, J. A., & Wadsworth, G. (2007). Family implementation of positive behavior support for a child with autism: Longitudinal, single-case, experimental, and descriptive replication and extension. *Journal of Positive Behavior Interventions, 9*, 131–150.

Lynch, E. W. (2011). Developing cross-cultural competence. In E. W. Lynch & M. J. Hanson (Eds.), *Developing cross-cultural competence—A guide for working with children and their families* (4th ed., pp. 41–77). Baltimore, MD: Paul H. Brookes.

Marulis, L. M., & Neuman, S. B. (2010). The effects of vocabulary intervention on young children's word learning: A meta-analysis. *Review of Educational Research, 80*, 300–335.

Matson, J. L. & Nebel-Schwalm, M. (2007). Assessing challenging behaviors in children with autism spectrum disorders: A review. *Research in Developmental Disabilities, 28*, 567–579.

McWilliam, R. A. (2010). *Routines-based early intervention: Supporting young children with special needs and their families.* Baltimore, MD: Brookes.

Meadan, H., Snodgrass, M. R., Meyer, L. E., Fisher, K. W., Chung, M. Y., & Halle, J. W. (2016). Internet-based parent-implemented intervention for young children with autism: A pilot study. *Journal of Early Intervention, 38*(1), 3–23.

Neitzel, J. (2010). Antecedent-based interventions for children and youth with autism spectrum disorder: Online training module. (Chapel Hill, NC: National Professional Development Center on Autism Spectrum Disorders, FPG Child Development Institute, UNC-Chapel Hill.) In Ohio Center for autism and Low Incidence (OCALI), *Autism Internet Modules*, www.autisminternetmodules.org. OH: OCALI.

Neitzel, J., & Wolery, M. (2010). Prompting for children and youth with autism spectrum disorders: Online training module. (Chapel Hill: National Professional Development Center on Autism Spectrum Disorders, FPG Child Development Institute, UNC-Chapel Hill). In Ohio Center for Autism and Low Incidence (OCALI), *Autism Internet Modules*, www.autismeinternetmodules.org. Columbus, OH: OCALI

O'Donnell, C. L. (2008). Defining, conceptualizing, and measuring fidelity of implementation and its relationship to outcomes in K–12 curriculum intervention research. *Review of Educational Research, 78*(1), 33–84.

Oliver, P., & Brady, M. P. (2014). Effects of covert audio coaching on parents' interactions with young children with autism. *Behavior Analysis in Practice, 7*(2), 112–116.

Phetrasuwan, S., Miles, M. S., and Mesibov, G. B. (2009). Defining autism spectrum disorders. *Journal for Specialists in Pediatric Nursing, 14*(3), 206–209.

Powell, D. & Dunlap, G. (2010). *Family-Focused Interventions for Promoting Social-Emotional Development in Infants and Toddlers with or at Risk for Disabilities.* Roadmap to Effective Intervention Practices #5. Tampa, Florida: University of South Florida, Technical Assistance Center on Social Emotional Intervention for Young Children.

Powell, D., Dunlap, G., & Fox, L. (2006). Prevention and intervention for the challenging behaviors of toddlers and preschoolers. *Infants & Young Children, 19*(1), 25–35.

Ruble, L., Mcgrew, J. H., & Toland, M. D. (2012). Goal attainment scaling as an outcome measure in randomized controlled trials of psychosocial interventions in autism. *Journal of Autism and Developmental Disorders, 42*(9), 1974–83.

Rush, D., & Shelden, M. (2011). *The early childhood coaching handbook.* Baltimore, MD: Paul H. Brookes Publishing Company.

Sam, A., & AFIRM Team (2015a). *Prompting.* Chapel Hill, NC: National Professional Development Center on Autism Spectrum Disorder, FPG Child Development Center, University of North Carolina. Retrieved from http://afirm.fpg.unc/prompting

Sam, A., & AFIRM Team (2015b). *Time delay.* Chapel Hill, NC: National Professional Development Center on Autism Spectrum Disorder, FPG Child Development Center, University of North Carolina. Retrieved from http://afirm.fpg.unc.edu/time-delay

Sam, A., & AFIRM Team (2015c). *Visual supports.* Chapel Hill, NC: National Professional Development Center on Autism Spectrum Disorder, FPG Child Development Center, University of North Carolina. Retrieved from http://afirm.fpg.unc.edu/visual-supports

Sam, A., & AFIRM Team. (2016). *Antecedent-based intervention.* Chapel Hill, NC: National Professional Development Center on Autism Spectrum Disorder, FPG Child Development Center, University of North Carolina. Retrieved from http://afirm.fgp.unc.edu/antecedent-based-intervention

Savage, M. N., & AFIRM Team (2017). *Differential reinforcement.* Chapel Hill, NC: National Professional Development Center on Autism Spectrum Disorder, FPG Child Development Center, University of North Carolina. Retrieved from http://afirm.fpg.unc.edu/differential-reinforcement

Scheeler, M. C., Bruno, K., Grubb, E., & Seavey, T. L. (2009). Generalizing teaching techniques from university to K-12 classrooms: Teaching preservice teachers to use what they learn. *Journal of Behavioral Education, 18*, 189–210.

Scheeler, M. C., Congdon, M., & Stansbery, S. (2010). Providing immediate feedback to co-teachers through bug-in-ear technology: an effective method of peer coaching in inclusion classrooms. *Teacher Education and Special Education, 33*, 83–96.

Shonkoff, J. P. & Phillips, D. A. (Eds.). (2000). *From neurons to neighborhoods: The science of early childhood development*. Washington, DC: National Academy Press.

Smith, S. M. (2008). Visual supports: Online training module (Columbus: Ohio Center for Autism and Low Incidence). In Ohio Center for Autism and Low Incidence (OCALI), *Autism Internet Modules*, www.autisminternetmodules.org. Columbus, OH: OCALI.

Vismara, L., Bogin, J., & Sullivan, L. (2010). Differential reinforcement: Online training module. (Sacramento, CA: National Professional Development Center on Autism Spectrum Disorders, M.I.N.D. Institute, University of California Davis). In Ohio Center for Autism and low Incidence (OCALI), *Autism Internet Modules*, www.autisminternetmodules.org. Columbus, OH: OCALI.

Wainer, A. L., & Ingersoll, B. R. (2013). Disseminating ASD interventions: A pilot study of a distance learning program for parents and professionals. *Journal of Autism and Developmental Disorders, 43*(1), 11–24.

Wainer, A. L., & Ingersoll, B. R. (2015). Increasing access to an ASD imitation intervention via a telehealth parent training program. *Journal of Autism and Developmental Disorders, 45*(12), 3877–3890.

Wong, C., Odom, S. L., Hume, K. A., Cox, A. W., Fettig, A., Kucharczyk, S., … Schultz, T. R. (2015). Evidence-based practices for children, youth, and young adults with Autism Spectrum Disorder: A comprehensive review. *Journal of Autism and Developmental Disorders, 45*(7), 1951–1966.

# Effects of Parent-Implemented Interventions on Outcomes for Children with Developmental Disabilities: A Meta-Analysis

*Tina Taylor Dyches, Timothy B. Smith, Byran B. Korth,
and Barbara Mandleco*

## Abstract

A large body of literature exists related to parent-implemented interventions for children with disabilities, so it is helpful to synthesize the results of outcome-based interventions for children with developmental disabilities. Specifically, what are the effects of parent-implemented interventions intended to improve children's (1) social behaviors, (2) life skills/adaptive behavior, and (3) communication skills? Using meta-analytic aggregation of effect sizes across 30 studies with a total of 1,356 participants, this review examined the association between parent-implemented interventions and intended outcomes for young children with developmental disabilities. Across all 30 studies comparing children's outcomes to control groups, the random-effects-weighted average effect size was $d = 0.495$ (95% confidence interval = 0.31 to 0.68). Effect sizes ranged from d = -0.28 to 3.23, with the index of heterogeneity reaching statistical significance ($Q = 72.0, p < .001; I^2 = 59.7\%$). The overall results were not moderated by the four participant characteristics evaluated—age, gender, socioeconomic status (SES), and disability. All parent-implemented interventions resulted in child outcomes that were statistically significantly better than the control group. Interventions targeting communication skills resulted in the greatest relative gains, and interventions targeting life skills/adaptive behavior resulted in the smallest relative gains (yet statistically better than the control group). Findings indicate clinical benefits when professionals include parents in interventions intended to influence the social-behavioral, communication, and adaptive development of young children with developmental disabilities.

Keywords: developmental disabilities, parent-implemented interventions, parent-mediated interventions, communication, social-emotional development, adaptive behavior, meta-analysis

# Background

Parents are considered "one of the most important influences in positive child and youth development" (Family Strengthening Policy Center, 2007, p. 1), and their influence on children with disabilities has been examined for many decades. For example, many studies investigated the use and effectiveness of programs for parents of children with various developmental disabilities (DD) including Down syndrome, autism spectrum disorders (ASD), and intellectual disabilities (Ainbinder et al., 1998; Bidder, Bryant, & Gray, 1975; Hudson et al., 2003; Schultz, Schmidt, & Stichter, 2011; Tonge et al., 2006). Parent-implemented interventions provided to these children are particularly relevant due to the emotional/behavioral challenges children with DD often exhibit, and the ways these challenges may increase the stressors and caregiving demands their parents experience (Azad, Blacher, & Marcoulides, 2013; Dabrowska & Pisula, 2010; Hayes & Watson, 2013; Woodman & Hauser-Cram, 2013; Xiong et al., 2011). Such stressors may also impact parents' ability to provide appropriate interventions.

Early, intensive, evidence-based interventions were shown to prevent future difficulties in children and their families (e.g., Benzies, Magill-Evans, Hayden, & Ballantyne, 2013; Durlak & Wells, 1997; Kovshoff, Hastings, & Remington, 2011). However, the relevant literature is either fragmented or has not been synthesized in a recent systematic review related to parent-implemented interventions and specific outcomes for the social behaviors, communication skills, and adaptive behavior of young children with disabilities. The severity of child impairment in these skills significantly impacts parental well-being, regardless of the type of child disability (e.g., Smith, Oliver, & Innocenti, 2001). Hence, to improve prevention efforts involving parents, a meta-analytic review examining the relationship between parent-implemented interventions and outcomes for children with DD is warranted.

## Parent-Implemented Interventions

Parenting interventions include a range of programs directed at "promoting positive outcomes or preventing negative outcomes for children via improvements in malleable parenting cognitions and/or practices identified in prior developmental research as significant contributors to children's outcomes" (Powell, 2013, pp. 266–267). Parent-implemented interventions involve training parents to provide interventions intended to improve the well-being of their children and prevent declines in child and family functioning. Beginning in the late 1950s, research on parent-implemented interventions has since proliferated. This body of literature was synthesized for parents of typically developing children, as well as for parents of children with various disabilities, mental health disorders, developmental delays, and children who are at risk of failure (de Graaf, Speetjens, Smit, de Wolff, & Tavecchio, 2008; Tellegen & Sanders, 2013).

More specific meta-analytic research and reviews investigated parent-implemented interventions for children with certain disabilities such as attention deficit hyperactivity disorder (ADHD; Corcoran & Dattalo, 2006; Lee, Nieuw, Yang, Chen, & Lin, 2012), ASD (McConachie & Diggle, 2007; Meadan, Ostrosky, Zaghlawan, & Yu, 2009; Oono, Honey, & McConachie, 2013; Schultz et al., 2011), cerebral palsy (Whittingham, Wee, & Boyd, 2011), DD (Singer, Ethridge, & Aldana, 2007), emotional-behavioral problems or disabilities (de Graaf et al., 2008), language impairments (Roberts & Kaiser, 2011), and even parents who themselves have intellectual disabilities (Coren, Thomae, & Hutchfield, 2011; Wade, Llewellyn, & Matthews, 2008).

## Results of Parent-Implemented Interventions

Although most meta-analyses on parent-implemented interventions focus on various parental outcomes such as parental stress (Singer et al., 2007), parental perceptions (Corcoran & Dattalo, 2006; Lee et al., 2012), parenting style (Tellegen & Sanders, 2013), and parental knowledge (McConachie & Diggle, 2007), relatively few focus directly on specific outcomes for children with disabilities. However, when child factors are analyzed, reports typically were limited to the effects of parent training on child maladaptive behavior (Lee et al., 2012; Corcoran & Dattalo, 2006; Schultz et al., 2011; Tellegen & Sanders, 2013; Whittingham et al., 2011) and communication skills (McConachie & Diggle, 2007; Meadan et al., 2009; Roberts & Kaiser, 2011). Analyses on social and life skill outcomes appear to be rare. On the other hand, given parents' ability to positively influence their children's behavior and communication skills, there is a strong likelihood that they might also have a significant impact on other areas of concern.

Research reviews and meta-analyses were also conducted on specific parenting programs as well (Petrenko, 2013). Results indicated parents' positive parenting styles and competency increased while parenting difficulties and child disruptive behaviors decreased (de Graaf et al., 2008; Tellegen & Sanders, 2013; Thomas & Zimmer-Gembeck, 2007). A study of five meta-analyses found early intensive behavioral intervention (EIBI) for young children with ASD to be an effective intervention to improve IQ and adaptive behavior; however, a possible publication and selection bias in these studies might confound the results (Reichow, 2012).

Taken together, the current body of literature related to the effects of parent-implemented interventions on specific outcomes for children with DD is limited. Also, the magnitude of the association remains uncertain, and factors moderating the association should be identified. Therefore, the purposes of the current meta-analysis were to aggregate the existing data quantitatively to yield an overall estimate of the association, and to analyze several variables likely impacting that association, based upon the following research questions: (a) Are parent-implemented interventions reliably related to specific child outcomes for children with developmental disabilities? and (b) What child and study variables moderate the association between parent-implemented interventions and child outcomes?

# Method

## Literature Search

Three primary concepts of interest to this investigation informed the search criteria: (a) interventions provided by parents of (b) children diagnosed with DD that would significantly impede their functioning, which resulted in (c) functional and measurable outcomes related to the children's disabilities, regardless of the location of delivery (e.g., home, clinic, school), or other aspects of the intervention (e.g., extent of training, duration, and intensity of intervention). DDs are those identified by the Developmental Disabilities Act of 2000, and include disabilities that result in "substantial functional limitations" in at least three areas of major life activity (e.g., receptive and expressive language, self-direction, capacity for independent living). Examples of possible DD (if the criteria are met) include ASD, intellectual disabilities, developmental delays, and genetic conditions such as Down syndrome.

First, we conducted extensive literature searches to obtain published and unpublished studies (i.e., journal articles, book chapters, doctoral dissertations, and master's theses) of interventions with children with DD explicitly involving parents as interventionists. We searched several electronic databases for articles written in English between 1990–2011: Academic Search Premier, Cumulative Index to Nursing and Allied Health Literature (CINAHL), Education Resources Information Center (ERIC), Medline, PsychINFO, and Social Sciences Abstracts. In each database we sought manuscripts with all three concepts of parent-implemented interventions, children with DD, and child outcomes. Search terms consisted of lists of synonyms separated by the Boolean "or" operator (with word stems to identify all word variants), including: (a) parent, mother, father, caregiver, etc. for the concept of parent; (b) child, infant, youth, etc. for the concept of children; (c) exceptional, disable, impair, special, autism, etc. for the concept of disability; and (d) intervene, treatment, sessions, training, etc. for the concept of interventions. We narrowed hits to those involving quantitative data by using a long list of inclusion terms, such as data, participants, research, results, statistic, and subjects. To ensure we located as many articles as possible, we searched the electronic databases three times using slight variations in search terms and keywords.

Database searches yielded 4,449 initial hits. Following this search, we reviewed titles and abstracts to verify the manuscripts met the inclusion criteria. Because we were interested in parent-implemented interventions for developmental disabilities that substantially impact several areas of life functioning typically evident in young children, we did not include studies with children with mild disabilities that primarily affect academic progress in school (e.g., ADHD, specific learning disability [SLD], behavior disorder) or with strictly physical disabilities (e.g., cerebral palsy without intellectual deficits, hearing impairments, visual impairments). The intervention provided had to be clearly relevant to the child's developmental condition, with an outcome measure aligning with the condition targeted in the intervention (e.g., a measure of expressive communication administered in a study of the effectiveness of an intervention intended to improve the child's expressive communication).

Subsequent reviews yielded 265 full manuscripts that were then examined to verify whether an effect size could be extracted. We sought studies involving experimental designs. Case studies, single-subject designs, qualitative research articles, and studies in which no actual parent-child interactions occurred were excluded. We did not exclude research reports based on subjective evaluations of research quality because no report appeared to be of such poor quality as to be excluded, and we were interested in describing the entire corpus of literature available on the topic (Glass, McGaw, & Smith, 1981; Rosenthal, 1991).

## Data Coding

Teams of two members each were trained to code data and verify the accuracy of coding. Each article was coded twice by separate teams, with the second coding team assessing the data of the first team for purposes of verification and correction of inaccuracies. Coders extracted independent and identifiable characteristics from each study, including (a) the number of child participants and their age, gender, and type of disability; (b) the age and gender of the parent(s); (c) the type, duration, and frequency of the intervention provided; (d) the type of research design and control group used; and (e) the effect size calculated using statistics provided within the manuscript.

Adequate inter-rater agreement was obtained for categorical variables (average Cohen's Kappa value of .74) and for continuous variables (average intraclass correlation value of .86 using one-way random effects models for single measures). Discrepancies among coding teams were resolved through further scrutiny of the manuscript to the point of consensus among coders.

## Computation of Effect Size Estimates

Among the studies included in this meta-analysis, several different statistics were reported: analyses of variance (ANOVAs), *t*-tests, odds ratios, chi squares, means and standard deviations, and *p*-values. In order to compare these data across studies, the statistics reported were converted into the metric of Cohen's d using the Meta-analysis Calculator software (Lyons & Morris, 2017). When an analysis was reported to be statistically significant, but no statistic was provided, the *d* value was determined by the corresponding *alpha* level (assuming two-tailed *alpha* = .05 unless reported otherwise). Analyses that reported results as non-significant, but gave no additional information were set to effect size $d = 0$. These procedures yielded conservative effect size estimates. The direction of all effect sizes was coded uniformly, such that positive values indicated a comparatively greater benefit to child outcomes as a function of the intervention provided, and negative values indicated a comparatively deleterious effect upon the child as a result of the parenting intervention relative to the control group.

Several studies reported data on multiple outcome measures. For example, some studies assessed several types of child social behavior (e.g., externalizing behaviors, appropriate eye contact). According to the assumption of statistically independent samples, there would be a greater likelihood of non-independence in the data should each effect size be used in the omnibus analysis (Cooper, 1998; Cooper, Hedges, & Valentine, 2009; Hedges & Olkin, 1985). Therefore, we averaged the effect sizes within each study (weighted by the number of participants included in the analysis) to compute an aggregate effect size (Mullen, 1989), so each study contributed only one data point in the omnibus analysis. We used random effects models to analyze the data (weighting effect sizes by the inverse of their variance) (Field, 2005).

Studies also reported effect sizes using several types of measures of child outcomes, and we sought to evaluate possible differences in the effectiveness of the interventions measured by a corresponding child outcome. We originally classified effect sizes within studies pertaining to child positive/pro-social behaviors, behavior problems, communication skills, and life skills/adaptive behaviors with the intention of analyzing the differences between the corresponding effect sizes using multivariate meta-analysis (Becker, 2000). Multivariate meta-analysis simultaneously evaluates the several types of dependent variable used within studies, but in this instance, after coding all studies there were no cases in which behavioral problems and life skills/adaptive behaviors were measured in the same study. To conduct the desired multivariate analysis, we therefore collapsed the two categories of positive/

pro-social behaviors and behavior problems by averaging those values (weighed by the number of participants) because those two categories were the most conceptually similar, sharing a comparable continuum, with the absence of positive/pro-social behaviors denoting behavioral problems (and vice versa) and the effect sizes from these two categories were highly correlated (above .90) with no significant difference between the mean values ($d = .42$ and $d = .44$, respectively). Thus, our multivariate meta-analysis considered three categories of child social behaviors, life skills/adaptive behaviors, and communication skills, accounting for the observed value of $r = 0.85$ for within study correlations.

# Results

## Descriptive Characteristics of Participants and Interventions

We located 52 studies with relevant data, but upon further inspection, 22 involved a single group of child participants evaluated from pre- to post-test (without a comparison/control group). Analyses of intervention effectiveness must account for the confounding variable of child maturation (Campbell & Stanley, 1966), so we focused our analyses on the 30 studies that compared children's outcomes to a control group (Table 1). This meta-analysis used the data from the 22 pre- to post-test studies solely for purpose of demonstrating that the results from that type of research design cannot be considered equivalent to the results of the 30 studies using quasi-experimental and experimental designs.

**Table 1 (Part 1).** *Overview of 30 Studies Included in the Meta-Analysis*

| Author(s) | N | Child Age[1] | Child Condition | Effect Size[2] |
|---|---|---|---|---|
| Aldred et al., 2004 | 28 | 4 | ASD | 1.02 |
| Bagner & Eyberg, 2007 | 22 | 5 | Intellectual disability | 1.04 |
| Boyce et al., 1993 | 51 | 4 | Multiple | .4 |
| Carter et al., 2011 | 62 | 2 | ASD | .00 |
| Chadwick et al., 2001 | 62 | 8 | Multiple | -.28 |
| Drew et al., 2002 | 24 | 2 | ASD | .61 |
| Feldman & Werner, 2002 | 36 | 11 | Multiple | .31 |
| Frankel et al., 2010 | 76 | 9 | ASD | .32 |
| Girolametto et al., 1994 | 14 | 2 | Multiple | 1.70 |
| Girolametto et al., 1998 | 12 | 3 | DS | .71 |
| Green et al., 2010 | 152 | 4 | ASD | .18 |
| Jocelyn et al., 1998 | 35 | 4 | ASD | .36 |
| Kasari et al., 2010 | 38 | 3 | ASD | .54 |
| Keen et al., 2010 | 39 | 3 | ASD | .30 |
| McConachie et al., 2005 | 51 | 3 | Developmental delay | .31 |
| Montgomery et al., 2004 | 66 | 2-9 | Mental retardation | .81 |
| Oosterling et al., 2010 | 75 | 3 | ASD | .31 |
| Pilarz, 2009 | 26 | 3-12 | ASD | 3.23 |
| Plant & Sanders, 2007 | 74 | 5 | Multiple | .67 |
| Quinn et al., 2007 | 31 | 5 | Multiple | .33 |
| Roberts et al., 2006 | 47 | 4 | Multiple | 1.02 |
| Roberts et al., 2011 | Varied | 4 | ASD | -.07 |
| Sofronoff et al., 2004 | 51 | 9 | Asperger syndrome | 1.11 |
| Sofronoff et al., 2007 | 45 | 11 | Asperger syndrome | 1.18 |
| Solomon et al., 2008 | 19 | 8 | ASD | .55 |
| Stahmer & Gist, 2001 | 22 | 3 | ASD | .15 |
| Strauss et al., 2012 | Varied | Varied | ASD | .17 |
| Wade et al., 2006 | 32 | 11 | Traumatic brain injury | .38 |
| Wong & Queenie, 2010 | 17 | 2 | ASD | .43 |
| Yoder & Warren, 2002 | 39 | 2 | Multiple | .00 |

*Note: 1 = average child age at first assessment; 2 = Cohen's d. NR = not reported; ASD = autism spectrum disorder; Con. = control group; DD = developmental disabilities; DS = Down syndrome; Exp. = experimental group; F = fathers; ID = intellectual disabilities; LI = language impairment; M = mothers; NRCT = non-randomized controlled trials; OS = observational study; P = parents, PDD = pervasive developmental disorder; RCT = randomized controlled trials; SES = socioeconomic status; TBI = traumatic brain injury.*

**Table 1 (Part 2).** *Overview of 30 Studies Included in the Meta-Analysis*

| Authors | Design | Design (P/M/F) | Subjects (SES) | Subjects (% White) |
|---|---|---|---|---|
| Aldred et al., 2004 | RCT | P | Middle class | 93% |
| Bagner & Eyberg, 2007 | RCT | M | No data | 67% |
| Boyce et al., 1993 | RCT | P | No data | No data |
| Carter et al., 2011 | RCT | P | Mixed | 47.4% |
| Chadwick et al., 2001 | RCT | P | No data | No data |
| Drew et al., 2002 | RCT | P | No data | No data |
| Feldman & Werner, 2002 | OS | P | Middle class | No data |
| Frankel et al., 2010 | RCT | P | No data | 45%. |
| Girolametto et al., 1994 | RCT | M | No data | No data |
| Girolametto et al., 1998 | RCT | M | Middle class | No data |
| Green et al., 2010 | RCT | P | Middle class | 57% |
| Jocelyn et al., 1998 | RCT | P | No data | 94% |
| Kasari et al., 2010 | RCT | P | No data | 58% |
| Keen et al., 2010 | pre-post test quisi-experimental design | P | No data | No data |
| McConachie et al., 2005 | NRCT | P | No data | No data |
| Montgomery et al., 2004 | RCT | P | No data | No data |
| Oosterling et al., 2010 | RCT | P | Mixed | No data |
| Pilarz, 2009 | NRCT | P | No data | No data |
| Plant & Sanders, 2007 | RCT | P | Mixed | No data |
| Quinn et al., 2007 | NRCT | P | Mixed | No data |
| Roberts et al., 2006 | RCT | P | No data | No data |
| Roberts et al., 2011 | RCTs/OSs | P | Varied | Varied |
| Sofronoff et al., 2004 | RCT | P | No data | No data |
| Sofronoff et al., 2007 | RCT | P | No data | No data |
| Solomon et al., 2008 | Matched-pairs design | P | Mixed | No data |
| Stahmer & Gist, 2001 | RCT | P | Mixed | No data |
| Strauss et al., 2012 | Varied | P | Varied | Varied |
| Wade et al., 2006 | RCT | P | No data | 81.3% |
| Wong & Queenie, 2010 | RCT | P | No data | No data |
| Yoder & Warren, 2002 | RCT | P | Slightly below national average | 48% |

**Table 1 (Part 3). *Overview of 30 Studies Included in the Meta-Analysis***

| Authors | Children with Disabilities Disability | Children with Disabilities Age in months | Sample Size Exp. [n] | Sample Size Con. [n] |
|---|---|---|---|---|
| Aldred et al., 2004 | ASD | 29–71 | 14 | 14 |
| Bagner & Eyberg, 2007 | Mental Retardation | 52.4 (mean) | 10 | 12 |
| Boyce et al., 1993 | Multiple | 47.15 (mean) | 26 | 25 |
| Carter et al., 2011 | ASD | 20.25 (mean) | 32 | 30 |
| Chadwick et al., 2001 | Cerebral palsy, DS; ASD | 96.4 (mean) | 38 | 24 |
| Drew et al., 2002 | ASD | 22.5 (mean) | 12 | 12 |
| Feldman & Werner, 2002 | DD | 132.5 (mean) | 18 | 18 |
| Frankel et al., 2010 | ASD | 2-5th grade | 40 | 36 |
| Girolametto et al., 1994 | DS;DD | 28.5 (mean) | 7 | 7 |
| Girolametto et al., 1998 | DS | 38.2 (mean) | 6 | 6 |
| Green et al., 2010 | ASD | 24-59 | 77 | 75 |
| Jocelyn et al., 1998 | ASD;PDD | 24-72 | 16 | 19 |
| Kasari et al., 2010 | ASD | 30.82 (mean) | 19 | 19 |
| Keen et al., 2010 | ASD | 36.05 (mean) | 17 | 22 |
| McConachie et al., 2005 | ASD | 36.54 (mean) | 26 | 25 |
| Montgomery et al., 2004 | Mental Retardation | 27-101 | 42 | 24 |
| Oosterling et al., 2010 | ASD | 34.4 (mean) | 40 | 35 |
| Pilarz, 2009 | ASD | 36-144 | 13 | 13 |
| Plant & Sanders, 2007 | Mixed | 55.10 (mean) | 50 | 24 |
| Quinn et al., 2007 | ASD; ID | 48-84 | 16 | 15 |
| Roberts et al., 2006 | Mixed | 51.78 (mean) | 27 | 20 |
| Roberts et al., 2011 | ASD; LI; DD | 18-60 | Varied | Varied |
| Sofronoff et al., 2004 | Asperger Syndrome | 112 (mean) | 36 | 15 |
| Sofronoff et al., 2007 | Asperger Syndrome | 129.4 (mean) | 24 | 21 |
| Solomon et al., 2008 | ASD | 97.8 (mean) | 10 | 9 |
| Stahmer & Gist, 2001 | ASD | 35.3 (mean) | 11 | 11 |
| Strauss et al., 2012 | ASD | 18-120 | Varied | Varied |
| Wade et al., 2006 | Pediatric TBI | 129.9 (mean) | 16 | 16 |
| Wong & Queenie, 2010 | ASD | 26.6 (mean) | 9 | 8 |
| Yoder & Warren, 2002 | ID | 22 (median) | 20 | 19 |

## Table 1 (Part 4). *Overview of 30 Studies Included in the Meta-Analysis*

| Author(s) | Intervention Name | Intervention Format |
|---|---|---|
| Aldred et al., 2004 | Child's Talk | Couple |
| Bagner & Eyberg, 2007 | Parent-child interaction therapy | Individual |
| Boyce et al., 1993 | Parent involvement component to center based program | Group |
| Carter et al., 2011 | Hanen's More Than Words | Group/individual |
| Chadwick et al., 2001 | Parent training Programs for children with behaviour problems | Group/individual |
| Drew et al., 2002 | Social-pragmatic joint attention focused parent training programme | Couple |
| Feldman & Werner, 2002 | Behavioral parent training (BPT) | Individual |
| Frankel et al., 2010 | Children's Friendship Training (CFT) | Couple |
| Girolametto et al., 1994 | Hanen Early Language Program | Group/individual |
| Girolametto et al., 1998 | Hanen Language Program | Individual |
| Green et al., 2010 | Preschool autism communication trial | Family |
| Jocelyn et al., 1998 | Autism preschool program | Group |
| Kasari et al., 2010 | Joint attention intervention | Couple |
| Keen et al., 2010 | Parent-focused intervention for children with a recent ASD diagnosis | Couple |
| McConachie et al., 2005 | More Than Words Program | Group |
| Montgomery et al., 2004 | Sleep intervention | Individual |
| Oosterling et al., 2010 | Focus parent training | Group/individual |
| Pilarz, 2009 | DIR/floor time parent training program for parents | Couple/individual |
| Plant & Sanders, 2007 | Stepping Stones Triple P | Individual |
| Quinn et al., 2007 | Parent Plus Programme | Group |
| Roberts et al., 2006 | Stepping Stones Triple P | Individual |
| Roberts et al., 2011 | Parent-implemented language interventions (meta-analysis) | Varied |
| Sofronoff et al., 2004 | Parent management training | Group/individual |
| Sofronoff et al., 2007 | Cognitive behavioural intervention for anger management | Group |
| Solomon et al., 2008 | Parent-child interaction therapy | Individual or couple |
| Stahmer & Gist, 2001 | Accelerated parent education program | Group |
| Strauss et al., 2012 | Meta-analysis of early intensive behavioral intervention programs (EIBI) | Varied |
| Wade et al., 2006 | Family-centered problem-solving intervention (FPS) | Group/individual |
| Wong & Queenie, 2010 | Autism 1-2-3 early intervention | Couple |
| Yoder & Warren, 2002 | Responsivity education combined with Prelinguistic Milieu Teaching (RPMT) | Individual |

## Table 1 (Part 5). *Overview of 30 Studies Included in the Meta-Analysis*

| Author(s) | Intervention Providers | Weeks/Sessions/Minutes | Relevant Dependent Variables |
|---|---|---|---|
| Aldred et al., 2004 | Parents | 26 weeks, 6 sess., 60 min. | Adaptive behavior |
| Bagner & Eyberg, 2007 | Mothers | 12 weeks, 12 sess., 60 min. | Maladaptive behavior |
| Boyce et al., 1993 | Parents | 15 weeks, 15 sess., 150 minutes | Adaptive behavior, communication |
| Carter et al., 2011 | Parents | 36 weeks, 11 sess., min. varied | Adaptive behavior, communication |
| Chadwick et al., 2001 | Parents; Teachers | Parents: 5-14 weeks, 5-7 sess., 60-120 min.; Teachers: 2-day training program | Maladaptive behavior |
| Drew et al., 2002 | Parents | 52 weeks, 4 activity checklists | Communication |
| Feldman & Werner, 2002 | Parents | 12-24 weeks, 12-24 sess., 60-120 min. | Maladaptive behavior |
| Frankel et al., 2010 | Parents | 12 weeks, 12 sess., 60 min. | Adaptive behavior |
| Girolametto et al., 1994 | Mothers | 12 weeks, 12 sess., 120 min. | Adaptive behavior, communication |
| Girolametto et al., 1998 | Mothers | 13 weeks, 13 sess., 150 min. | Communication |
| Green et al., 2010 | Parents | 52 weeks, 18 sess., 120 min. | Adaptive behavior, communication |
| Jocelyn et al., 1998 | Parents | 10 weeks, 30 sess., 60 min. | Adaptive behavior |
| Kasari et al., 2010 | Parents | 8 weeks, 24 sess., 30 min. | Adaptive behavior |
| Keen et al., 2010 | Parents | 6 weeks, 10 sess., 60 min. | Adaptive behavior, communication |
| McConachie et al., 2005 | Parents | 20 weeks, 20 sess., 60 min. | Adaptive behavior, communication, maladaptive behavior |
| Montgomery et al., 2004 | Parents | Varied | Adaptive behavior |
| Oosterling et al., 2010 | Parents | 104 weeks, 15 sess., 120-180 min. | Adaptive behavior, communication |
| Pilarz, 2009 | Parents | 7 weeks, 7 sess., 60 min. (first was 120) | Adaptive behavior, communication |
| Plant & Sanders, 2007 | Parents | 10-16 weeks, 10 sess., 60-90 min. | Maladaptive behavior |
| Quinn et al., 2007 | Parents | 6 weeks, 6 sess., 120 min. | Maladaptive behavior |
| Roberts et al., 2006 | Parents | 10 sess., 40-120 min. | Maladaptive behavior |
| Roberts et al., 2011 | Parents | Varied | Communication |
| Sofronoff et al., 2004 | Parents | Group: 1 day workshop; Individual: 6 weeks, 6 sess., 60 min. | Adaptive behavior, maladaptive behavior |
| Sofronoff et al., 2007 | Parents | 6 weeks, 6 sess., 60 min. | Maladaptive behavior |
| Solomon et al., 2008 | Parents | 12 sess. | Adaptive behavior, maladaptive behavior |
| Stahmer & Gist, 2001 | Parents | 12 weeks, 12 sess., 60 min. | Adaptive behavior |
| Strauss et al., 2012 | Parents | Varied | Adaptive behavior |
| Wade et al., 2006 | Parents | 26 weeks, 7-11 sess., 75-100 min. | Adaptive behavior, communication |
| Wong & Queenie, 2010 | Parents | 2 weeks, 10 sess., 30 min. | Adaptive behavior, communication |
| Yoder & Warren, 2002 | Parents | 26 weeks, 78-104 sess., 20 min. | Adaptive behavior, communication |

Across the 30 studies using quasi-experimental and experimental designs, 1,356 participants were recruited from hospitals and medical clinics (30%), early intervention clinics (20%), public schools (10%), community agencies/clinics (10%), or multiple sites (20%). The majority of the intervention studies were published after 2006, indicating a notable recent increase in parent intervention studies investigating child outcomes.

Across the 30 studies, the mean age of children at initial evaluation was 5.0 years (range = 2–11), with an average of only 20% being female. Most studies (n = 17; 57%) included children with ASD. Nine included children with mild to moderate delays, four included children with moderate to severe delays, and eight studies included children with a wide range of delays from mild to severe, with nine not providing information regarding the severity of the disability. The average age of the parent(s) was 35 years, with 25 studies (83%) involving mother and father, 3 studies involving only mothers, and 2 studies with multiple caregivers (e.g., parents and grandparents). On average, parents and caregivers studied were from middle class socioeconomic backgrounds, with only two studies limited to families from low socioeconomic backgrounds.

Interventions in these 30 studies involving parents varied substantially as to where they occurred: 7 were conducted in homes, 4 in clinical settings, and the remaining 19 in a variety of locations (e.g., home visits and clinic instruction). Nine interventions targeted child behaviors (e.g., aggression, social engagement), 4 targeted child communication skills (e.g., oral expression), and the remaining 17 interventions involved both of those foci and/or also included life skills/adaptive behaviors.

Child outcomes were measured several ways: 9 studies used direct observations, 9 asked parents to complete standardized instruments, 12 used a combination of direct observation and standardized instruments. The median parent training regimen occurred weekly for 12 weeks, with an average duration of 102 minutes (range = 30–180). Intervention sessions with children were most often conducted by parents (60%), but two studies had interventions provided by parents and professionals together, seven had interventions provided separately by the parents at home and professionals in the clinic, and two studies included multiple types of interventions with parents and professionals working both separately and together.

## Omnibus Analysis

Across all 30 studies comparing children's outcomes to control groups, the random effects weighted average size was $d = 0.495$

### Figure 1.
### *Forest Plot of Studies in the Meta-Analysis*

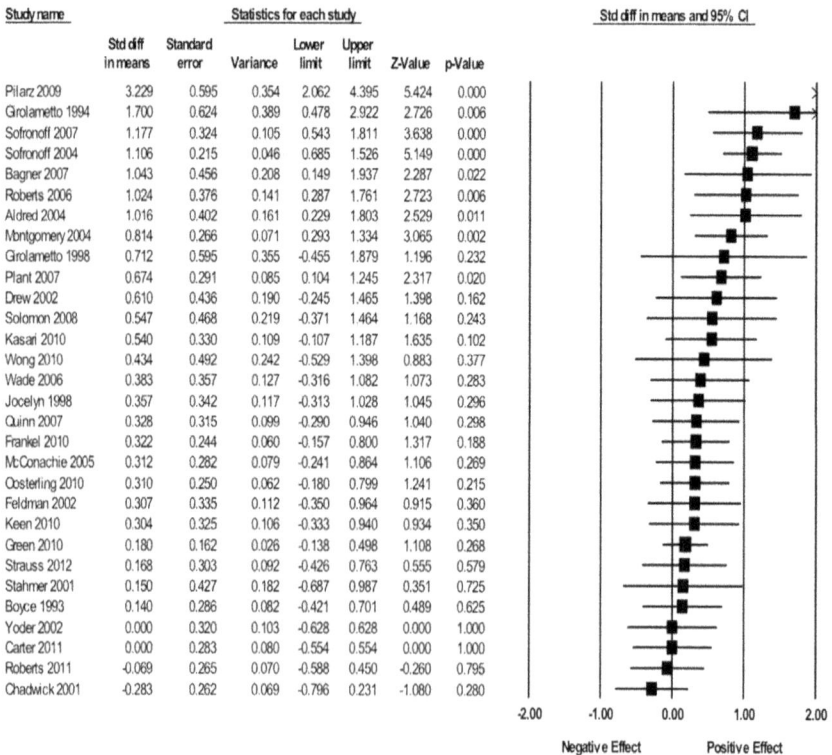

| Study name | Std diff in means | Standard error | Variance | Lower limit | Upper limit | Z-Value | p-Value |
|---|---|---|---|---|---|---|---|
| Pilarz 2009 | 3.229 | 0.595 | 0.354 | 2.062 | 4.395 | 5.424 | 0.000 |
| Girolametto 1994 | 1.700 | 0.624 | 0.389 | 0.478 | 2.922 | 2.726 | 0.006 |
| Sofronoff 2007 | 1.177 | 0.324 | 0.105 | 0.543 | 1.811 | 3.638 | 0.000 |
| Sofronoff 2004 | 1.106 | 0.215 | 0.046 | 0.685 | 1.526 | 5.149 | 0.000 |
| Bagner 2007 | 1.043 | 0.456 | 0.208 | 0.149 | 1.937 | 2.287 | 0.022 |
| Roberts 2006 | 1.024 | 0.376 | 0.141 | 0.287 | 1.761 | 2.723 | 0.006 |
| Aldred 2004 | 1.016 | 0.402 | 0.161 | 0.229 | 1.803 | 2.529 | 0.011 |
| Montgomery 2004 | 0.814 | 0.266 | 0.071 | 0.293 | 1.334 | 3.065 | 0.002 |
| Girolametto 1998 | 0.712 | 0.595 | 0.355 | -0.455 | 1.879 | 1.196 | 0.232 |
| Plant 2007 | 0.674 | 0.291 | 0.085 | 0.104 | 1.245 | 2.317 | 0.020 |
| Drew 2002 | 0.610 | 0.436 | 0.190 | -0.245 | 1.465 | 1.398 | 0.162 |
| Solomon 2008 | 0.547 | 0.468 | 0.219 | -0.371 | 1.464 | 1.168 | 0.243 |
| Kasari 2010 | 0.540 | 0.330 | 0.109 | -0.107 | 1.187 | 1.635 | 0.102 |
| Wong 2010 | 0.434 | 0.492 | 0.242 | -0.529 | 1.398 | 0.883 | 0.377 |
| Wade 2006 | 0.383 | 0.357 | 0.127 | -0.316 | 1.082 | 1.073 | 0.283 |
| Jocelyn 1998 | 0.357 | 0.342 | 0.117 | -0.313 | 1.028 | 1.045 | 0.296 |
| Quinn 2007 | 0.328 | 0.315 | 0.099 | -0.290 | 0.946 | 1.040 | 0.298 |
| Frankel 2010 | 0.322 | 0.244 | 0.060 | -0.157 | 0.800 | 1.317 | 0.188 |
| McConachie 2005 | 0.312 | 0.282 | 0.079 | -0.241 | 0.864 | 1.106 | 0.289 |
| Oosterling 2010 | 0.310 | 0.250 | 0.062 | -0.180 | 0.799 | 1.241 | 0.215 |
| Feldman 2002 | 0.307 | 0.335 | 0.112 | -0.350 | 0.964 | 0.915 | 0.360 |
| Keen 2010 | 0.304 | 0.325 | 0.106 | -0.333 | 0.940 | 0.934 | 0.350 |
| Green 2010 | 0.180 | 0.162 | 0.026 | -0.138 | 0.498 | 1.108 | 0.268 |
| Strauss 2012 | 0.168 | 0.303 | 0.092 | -0.426 | 0.763 | 0.555 | 0.579 |
| Stahmer 2001 | 0.150 | 0.427 | 0.182 | -0.687 | 0.987 | 0.351 | 0.725 |
| Boyce 1993 | 0.140 | 0.286 | 0.082 | -0.421 | 0.701 | 0.489 | 0.625 |
| Yoder 2002 | 0.000 | 0.320 | 0.103 | -0.628 | 0.628 | 0.000 | 1.000 |
| Carter 2011 | 0.000 | 0.283 | 0.080 | -0.554 | 0.554 | 0.000 | 1.000 |
| Roberts 2011 | -0.069 | 0.265 | 0.070 | -0.588 | 0.450 | -0.260 | 0.795 |
| Chadwick 2001 | -0.283 | 0.262 | 0.069 | -0.796 | 0.231 | -1.080 | 0.280 |

*Forest plot of effect size and 95% confidence interval of parent-mediated intervention efficacy for meta-analysis.*

(95% confidence interval $d = 0.31$ to 0.68). Effect sizes ranged from $d = -0.28$ to 3.23, with the index of heterogeneity reaching statistical significance ($Q = 72.0$, $p < .001$; $I^2 = 59.7\%$). Thus, the magnitude of the association between parent-implemented interventions and child variables was moderately inconsistent across studies, and we subsequently evaluated several possible moderating variables that could account for heterogeneity in the findings. Figure 1 shows the Forest plot of the calculated results with standardized effect size using the differences in means, standard error, and variance in the 30 selected studies.

## Assessment of Publication Bias

To evaluate whether the omnibus results were biased against the null hypothesis, we conducted several procedures to detect possible publication bias (Rosenthal, 1979). Publication bias can occur in a meta-analysis because studies with statistically significant results are more likely to be published than are studies with statistically non-significant results. Because published studies tend to be located more readily than unpublished studies, a meta-analysis failing to locate research studies with non-significant results (usually with a small number of participants) may yield excessively high estimates. When we examined the possibility of publication bias using Egger's regression test, it reached statistical significance ($p = .02$), suggesting abnormalities in effect size distribution, a possible indicator of publication bias. Subsequent inspection of the funnel-plot of the effect sizes (x-axis) by the inverse of the standard error of the effect size (y-axis) revealed a single study with a large effect size value ($d = 3.23$) made the data asymmetrical, but the rest of the data were distributed fairly evenly around the mean, suggesting a low probability of "missing" studies (Sutton, 2009). Furthermore, the omnibus effect size remained the same when subjected to trim and fill analyses (Duvall & Tweedie, 2000). Thus, publication bias did not appear to be a substantial threat to the results obtained in this meta-analysis.

## Moderation by Participant Characteristics

To investigate whether the effectiveness of the interventions varied as a function of participant characteristics, we conducted analyses involving average child age, child gender, family socioeconomic status, and type of disability. In order to establish whether differences in the age of the sample accounted for significant differences in between-studies variance, the effect sizes within studies were correlated with the average age of child participants in that study. The resulting random effects weighted correlation was .22 ($p > .05$), indicating a mildly positive, but statistically insignificant trend in effect size magnitude as a function of child age (greater relative gains tended to characterize studies with children older than the average age of 5 years). The correlations computed with the gender composition of the sample (percent female) and family socioeconomic status were of very small magnitude ($r = .01$ and -.07, respectively), indicating results obtained within studies did not differ as a function of these variables.

We next evaluated if results varied by type of disability. Because ASD was the only disability occurring with sufficient consistency across studies to conduct comparative analyses, we contrasted those studies with studies in which children had other types of disabilities (e.g., developmental delays, intellectual disabilities). The results of a random effects weighted analysis of variance ($Q = 0.1$, $p = .78$) indicated studies of children with ASD had essentially the same average effect sizes ($d = .52$) as studies of children with another form of disability ($d = .47$). Thus, the overall results presented earlier were not moderated by the four participant characteristics evaluated.

## Moderation by Intervention Characteristics

Because interventions differed in content, focus, and intensity, it was essential to evaluate those differences in terms of effectiveness. We first sought to determine whether the intervention effectiveness depended on the type of child outcome targeted by the intervention. This analysis entailed a multivariate meta-analysis in which three categories of child outcomes (social behaviors, life skills/adaptive behaviors, and communication skills) were compared simultaneously. The overall model reached statistical significance (Wald chi square = 27.3, $p < .0001$), with the results by type of intervention/outcome reported in Table 2. All three interventions resulted in child outcomes that were statistically significantly better than the alternative intervention (control group). Interventions targeting child communication skills resulted in the greatest relative gains, and interventions targeting child life skills/adaptive behavior resulted in the smallest relative gains (yet statistically better than the control group). Nevertheless, this difference between interventions and outcomes types could have been attributable to other factors, including the nature of the control group and intensity of the intervention provided, so it was important to evaluate those two variables to contextualize the results obtained.

### Table 2.
#### Weighted Mean Effect Sizes by Type of Child Outcome

| Child outcome targeted by intervention | k | d+ | se | 95 % CI |
|---|---|---|---|---|
| Social behaviors, positive and negative | 22 | .43 | .11 | [.21, .66] |
| Life skills/ adaptive behaviors | 7 | .35 | .13 | [.09, .60] |
| Communication skills | 14 | .60* | .12 | [.37, .83] |
| All outcomes combined | 30 | .50 | .09 | [.31, .68] |

Note: Effect sizes were derived from distinct types of child outcome measures that aligned with the type of intervention(s) provided within studies. k = number of studies. d+ = random effects weighted effect size (Cohen's d). se = standard error. * = statistically significantly different from Life Skills/Adaptive Behaviors (p < .05).

Studies most often (67%) involved control groups not receiving a comparable intervention (e.g., participants placed on a waiting list), and results from those 20 studies were compared to 10 studies in which children in the control group received a comparable intervention that did not involve parents (e.g., treatment as usual or a similar treatment administered by professionals rather than parents). Although differences did not reach statistical significance ($Q = 2.5, p = .11$), likely due to the small number of studies involved, the average random effects weighted effect size for the 10 studies with a comparable intervention administered to the control group ($d = .30$) was half the magnitude of the 20 studies without a comparable intervention administered to the control group ($d = .60$).

We next compared the results of all 30 intervention studies using a control group with results obtained from 22 studies mentioned earlier that did not use a control group (i.e., that evaluated child gains over time from pre- to post-test). The difference in effect size magnitude did not reach statistical significance ($Q = 1.7, p = .19$), but the 30 studies comparing outcomes to a control group were characterized by much less robust child outcomes ($d = .50$) compared to the 22 studies that did not account for child maturation and other confounds through the use of a control group ($d = .70$).

Finally, we evaluated whether or not the intervention intensity affected child outcomes across the 30 experimental studies. We found an unexpected negative correlation (random effects weighted) between the total amount of time spent on training parents (multiplying number of sessions by session duration) and the study effect size ($r = -.39$). This finding was counter-intuitive: interventions with extensive parent training (up to 30 total sessions) were less effective than interventions with moderate parent training (typically 12 sessions). This finding remained the same after statistically controlling for the severity of the child's disability, but it was partially explained by more rigorous studies having a comparable intervention administered to the control group (which had relatively lower effect sizes) also had more intensive parent training (an average of 68% more total time). When removing less intensive studies without a comparable intervention from the analysis, the correlation no longer reached statistical significance but was still of notable magnitude ($r = -.30$). This finding and several of the others clearly warrant careful interpretation.

## Discussion

The results of this meta-analysis demonstrated an overall beneficial effect of parent-implemented interventions with young children with DD. Across all 30 studies reviewed, the random effects weighted average effect size indicated a moderate, statistically significant effect, similar to results of other meta-analyses and reviews of interventions for children with various disabilities (de Graaf et al., 2008; Dunst, Trivette, & Hamby, 2007; McConachie & Diggle, 2007; Meadan et al., 2009; Reichow, 2012; Schultz et al., 2011; Singer et al., 2007; Tellegen & Sanders, 2013; Thomas & Zimmer-Gembeck, 2007). We found no meta-analyses indicating parent-implemented interventions were not effective in increasing child skill levels.

Our results indicate a clinical benefit of parent-implemented interventions, particularly when such interventions focus on child social behavioral, adaptive, and communication skills, as these focused interventions resulted in statistically significantly gains compared to control groups. However, effectiveness varied across the type of intervention provided. Specifically, children experienced greater gains in communication skills than in life skills/adaptive behavior, although this result remains tentative because only seven studies targeted adaptive behavior.

Moreover, when studies compared parent-directed interventions to interventions provided solely by professionals, the comparable effectiveness persisted. There is a clinical benefit of including parents in interventions that deserves sustained research attention (Mahoney et al., 1999) and practical implementation, particularly because emotional/behavioral challenges in early childhood are associated with similar challenges as children age (Saito et al., 2017). Early identification and intervention to treat emotional/behavioral challenges, especially for children with ASD, are warranted.

We were surprised the association between the amount of time spent training parents was inversely related to intervention effectiveness. Inspection of the scatterplot revealed extensive interventions were less effective in terms of child outcomes (relative to control groups) than interventions with an average number of about 12 sessions. This finding could have occurred for a number of reasons, and the relatively few number of studies analyzed cannot rule out sampling error as a reason. Furthermore, one could imagine multiple confounds. For example, the quality of the intervention is not necessarily related to quantity, and parents with children whose behavior had proven difficult to change in their previous attempts may have been more willing to participate in very extensive training. However, these possible confounds cannot be evaluated in a meta-analysis, which is reliant on descriptions provided by authors. Thus, the unexpected negative correlation remains uninterpretable, except to note extensive training for parents may not necessarily enhance child gains more than typical levels of training (about 12 sessions, 90 minutes weekly).

The overall magnitude of results did not differ as a function of child age or gender. Furthermore, although most of the studies included children with ASD (likely due to the increased prevalence and attention given to this population in the past two decades), the interventions were just as effective with children with ASD as with children with other disabilities. Thus, parent-led interventions can be effective with a variety of populations.

## Limitations

Because we located only 30 studies that aligned with the study's purpose and search criteria, it is likely the overall results may shift in the future as more empirical results can be aggregated. Furthermore, our search strategies may have missed some primarily parent-based articles if they did not use the keywords we used in our searches. In any case, this meta-analysis should not to be construed as definitive. A clear strength of the studies we reviewed was the common inclusion of both mothers and fathers, but a clear limitation is that most studies we reviewed involved young children, with children having ASD being overrepresented relative to other conditions. Hence, we do not know how parent interventions may work with older children or with specific conditions such as Down syndrome. Finally, on average, studies had 45 child participants, so results are subject to sampling error and have limited external validity; studies with more participants are warranted.

## Implications for Future Research

Several implications for future research are related to both study design and content. We suggest researchers conduct no future single group (pre- to post-test change) designs because those are highly problematic with children, subject to maturation effects. We found the average effect size of studies using the weaker design was 0.20 higher than studies using control groups, effectively changing the interpretation of results from a moderate effect ($d = .50$) to a strong effect ($d = .70$). Editors are advised not to accept manuscripts with that design unless maturation rates are controlled.

Future research should increase the sample size of intervention groups. The average number of participants was only 45 total children per study. Statistically, it would be optimal if at least 80 participants were evaluated.

Because the included studies had a restricted range of demographic characteristics, additional study is warranted to determine the mediating or moderating effects of level of functioning, comorbid challenging behaviors, gender, race/ethnicity, and socioeconomic status on treatment outcome.

Also, more studies should compare parent-based interventions to clinic-based interventions conducted by professionals and include treatment fidelity data (Schultz et al., 2011). With limited data available, it appears parent-based interventions may be more effective than comparable interventions conducted by professionals without parent involvement. However, the limited number of studies utilizing control groups receiving treatment limits confidence with which we can make that assertion.

The optimal effectiveness of training for parents of children with DD is not necessarily extensive. In fact, extensive parent training can be problematic from a research perspective (the longer the training, the greater likelihood of participant dropout) and from a practical perspective (e.g., parents facing many demands on their time). So future research should manipulate the depth and amount of training to provide recommendations regarding efficient yet effective practices. This is not to say interventions should be cut—the average study involved 18–20 hours of parent training spread out over 12 weeks—but it is saying when a program involves over 30 total hours, interventionists should carefully consider outcomes relative to intervention costs.

Finally, because many types of parent training exist, future research should examine the differences of various strategies on child outcomes. For example, some intervention programs train parents in the skills but do not provide coaching, modeling, or feedback related to the parents' actual implementation of strategies. Other programs may include the trainer observing the parent-child interaction, allowing the trainer to provide feedback. While some research exists in this area (Bearss et al., 2015; Fettig, Schultz, & Sreckovic, 2015), the type of training for parents of children with DD that is most effective and clinically significant is not definitive.

## Conclusions

This meta-analysis was an attempt to synthesize the literature regarding the relationship between parent-implemented interventions and communication, behavior, and adaptive skill outcomes for children with DD. Most studies in this meta-analysis included interventions primarily involving young boys with ASD (with mild/moderate delays), interventions provided by mothers and fathers from middle-class socioeconomic backgrounds in multiple environments, interventions involving weekly parent training over a 12-week period, and interventions focusing on multiple outcomes (social, communication, adaptive skills).

Results from this study indicate parent interventions make a difference in various outcomes for children with DD, and these effects are sustained over time. Providers focused on prevention may benefit from training parents of young children with DD to promote positive social responses from their children, and consider teaching both mothers and fathers interventions with long-term effects on child outcomes (Elder et al., 2011).

## References

(Entries marked with an * are included in the meta-analysis)

Ainbinder, J., Blanchard, L., Singer, G., Sullivan, M., Powers, L., Marquis, J., & Santelli, B. (1998). A qualitative study of parent to parent support for parents of children with special needs. *Journal of Pediatric Psychology, 23*, 99–109.

*Aldred, C., Green, J., & Adams, C. (2004). A new social communication intervention for children with autism: Pilot randomised controlled treatment study suggesting effectiveness. *Journal of Child Psychology and Psychiatry, 45*, 1420–1430.

Azad, G., Blacher, J., & Marcoulides, G. (2013). Mothers of children with developmental disabilities: Stress in early and middle childhood. *Research in Developmental Disabilities, 34*, 3449–3459.

*Bagner, D. M., & Eyberg, S. M. (2007). Parent-child interaction therapy for disruptive behavior in children with mental retardation: A randomized controlled trial. *Journal of Clinical Child and Adolescent Psychology, 36*, 418–429.

Bearss, K., Johnson, C., Smith, T., Lecavalier, L., Swiezy, N., Aman, M., ... Scahill, L. (2015). Effect of parent training vs. parent education on behavioral problems in children with autism spectrum disorder: A randomized clinical trial. *The Journal of the American Medical Association, 313*, 1524–2533.

Becker, B. J. (2000). Multivariate meta-analysis. In H. E. A. Tinsley & S. D. Brown (Eds.). *Handbook of Applied Multivariate Statistics and Mathematical Modeling* (pp. 499–525). San Diego, CA: Academic Press.

Benzies, K. M., Magill-Evans, J. E., Hayden, K. A., & Ballantyne, M. (2013). Key components of early intervention programs for preterm infants and their parents: A systematic review and meta-analysis. *BMC Pregnancy and Childbirth, 13*(1), S10.

Bidder, R., Bryant, G., & Gray, O. (1975). Benefits to Down's syndrome children through training their mothers. *Archives of Disease in Childhood, 50*, 383–386.

*Boyce, G. C., White, K. R., & Burton, K. (1993). The effectiveness of adding a parent involvement component to an existing center-based program for children with disabilities and their families. *Early Education and Development, 4*, 327–345.

Campbell, D. T., & Stanley, J. C. (1966). *Experimental and quasi-experimental designs for research*. Chicago, IL: Rand-McNally.

*Carter, A. S., Messinger, D. S., Stone, W. L., Celimi, S., Nahmias, A. S., & Yoder, P. (2011). A randomized controlled trial of Hanen's 'More Than Words' in toddlers with early autism symptoms. *Journal of Child Psychology and Psychiatry, 52*, 741–752.

*Chadwick, O., Momcilovic, N., Rossiter, R., Stumbles, E., & Taylor, E. (2001). A randomized trial of brief individual versus group parent training for behaviour problems in children with severe learning disabilities. *Behavioural and Cognitive Psychotherapy, 29*, 151–167.

Cooper, H. (1998). *Synthesizing research: A guide for literature reviews* (3rd ed.). Thousand Oaks, CA: Sage.

Cooper, H., Hedges, L. V, & Valentine, J. (Eds.). (2009). *The handbook of research synthesis and meta-analysis*. New York, NY: Russell Sage.

Corcoran, J., & Dattalo, P. (2006). Parent involvement in treatment for ADHD: A meta-analysis of the published studies. *Research on Social Work Practice, 16*, 561–570.

Coren, E., Thomae, M., & Hutchfield, J. (2011). Parent training for intellectually disabled parents: A Cochrane systematic review. *Research on Social Work Practice, 21*, 432–441.

Dabrowska, A., & Pisula, E. (2010). Parenting stress and coping styles in mothers and fathers of pre-school children with autism and Down syndrome. *Journal of Intellectual Disability Research, 54*, 266–80.

de Graaf, I., Speetjens, P., Smit, F., de Wolff, M., & Tavecchio, L. (2008). Effectiveness of the Triple P Positive Parenting Program on behavioral problems in children. *Behavior Modification, 32*, 714–735.

Developmental Disabilities Assistance and Bill of Rights Act of 2000, Pub L.106-402 (106th Congress, 2nd Sess.).

*Drew, A., Baird, G., Baron-Cohen, S., Cox, A., Slonims, V., Wheelwright, S., ... Charman, T. (2002). A pilot randomised control trial of a parent training intervention for pre-school children with autism: Preliminary findings and methodological challenges. *European Child and Adolescent Psychiatry, 11*, 266–272.

Dunst, C., Trivette, C., & Hamby, D. (2007). Meta-analysis of family-centered help giving practices research. *Mental Retardation and Developmental Disabilities Research Reviews, 13*, 370–378.

Durlak, J. A., & Wells, A. M. (1997). Primary prevention mental health programs for children and adolescents: A meta-analytic review. *American Journal of Community Psychology, 25*(2), 115–152.

Duvall, S., & Tweedie, R. (2000). Trim and fill: A simple funnel-plot-based method of testing and adjusting for publication bias in meta-analysis. *Biometrics, 56*, 455–463.

Elder, J. H., Donaldson, S. O., Kairalla, J., Valcante, G., Bendixen, R., Ferdig, R., … Serano, M. (2011). In-home training for fathers of children with autism: A follow up study and evaluation of four individual training components. *Journal of Child and Family Studies, 20*, 263–271.

Family Strengthening Policy Center. (2007). *The parenting imperative: Investing in parents so children and youth succeed*. Washington, DC: National Human Services Assembly.

*Feldman, M. A., & Werner, S. E. (2002). Collateral effects of behavioral parent training on families of children with developmental disabilities and behavior disorders. *Behavioral Interventions, 17*(2), 75–83.

Fettig, A., Schultz, T. R., Sreckovic, M. A. (2015). Effects of coaching on the implementation of functional assessment-based parent intervention in reducing challenging behaviors. *Journal of Positive Behavior Interventions, 17*, 170–180.

Field, A. P. (2005). Is the meta-analysis of correlation coefficients accurate when population correlations vary? *Psychological Methods, 10*(4), 444–467.

*Frankel, F., Myatt, R., Sugar, C., Witham, C., Gorospe, C. M., & Laugeson, E. (2010). A randomized controlled study of parent-assisted children's friendship training with children having autism spectrum disorders. *Journal of Autism Development Disorders, 40*, 827–842.

*Girolametto, L., Verbey, M., & Tannock, R. (1994). Improving joint engagement in parent-child interaction: An intervention study. *Journal of Early Intervention, 18*, 155–167.

*Girolametto, L., Weitzman, E., & Clements-Baartman, J. (1998). Vocabulary intervention for children with Down syndrome: Parent training using focused stimulation. *The Transdisciplinary Journal, 8*, 109–125.

Glass, G. V., McGaw, B., & Smith, M. L. (1981). *Meta-analysis in social research*. Thousand Oaks, CA: Sage.

*Green, J., Charman, T., McConachie, H., Aldred, C., Slonims, V., Howlin, P., & Pickles, A. (2010). Parent-mediated communication-focused treatment in children with autism (PACT): A randomised controlled trial. *Lancet, 375,* 2152–2160.

Hayes, S., & Watson, S. (2013). The impact of parenting stress: A meta-analysis of studies comparing the experience of parenting stress in parents of children with and without autism spectrum disorder. *Journal of Autism and Developmental Disorders, 43,* 629–642.

Hedges, L. V., & Olkin, I. (1985). *Statistical methods for meta-analysis.* New York, NY: Academic Press.

Hudson, A., Matthews, J., Gavidia-Payne, S., Cameron, C., Mildon, R., Radler, G., & Nankervis, K. (2003). Evaluation of an intervention system for parents of children with intellectual disability and challenging behaviour. *Journal of Intellectual Disability Research, 47,* 238–249.

*Jocelyn, L. J., Casiro, O. G., Beattie, D., Bow, J., & Kneisz, J. (1998). Treatment of children with autism: A randomized controlled trial to evaluate a caregiver-based intervention program in community day-care centers. *Journal of Developmental and Behavioral Pediatrics, 19,* 326–334.

*Kasari, C., Gulsrud, A. C., Wong, C., Kwon, S., & Locke, J. (2010). Randomized controlled caregiver mediated joint engagement intervention for toddlers with autism. *Journal of Autism and Developmental Disorders, 40,* 1045–1056.

*Keen, D., Couzens, D., Muspratt, S., & Rodger, S. (2010). The effects of a parent-focused intervention for children with a recent diagnosis of autism spectrum disorder on parenting stress and competence. *Research in Autism Spectrum Disorders, 4,* 229–241.

Kovshoff, H., Hastings, R. P., & Remington, B. (2011). Two-year outcomes for children with autism after the cessation of early intensive behavioral intervention. *Behavior Modification, 35,* 427–450.

Lee, P., Nieuw, W., Yang, H., Chen, V. C., & Lin, K. (2012). A meta-analysis of behavioral parent training for children with attention deficit hyperactivity disorder. *Research in Developmental Disabilities, 33,* 2040–2049.

Lyons, L. C., & Morris, W. A. (2017). The meta-analysis calculator [Computer software]. Manassas, VA: Author.

Mahoney, G., Kaiser, A., Girolametto, L., MacDonald, J., Robinson, C., Safford, P., & Spiker, D. (1999). Parent education in early intervention: A call for a renewed focus. *Topics in Early Childhood Special Education, 19,* 131–140.

McConachie, H., & Diggle, T. (2007). Parent implemented early intervention for young children with autism spectrum disorder: A systematic review. *Journal of Evaluation in Clinical Practice, 13,* 120–129.

*McConachie, H., Randle, V., Hammal, D., & Le Couteur, A. (2005). A controlled trial of a training course for parents of children with suspected autism spectrum disorder. *The Journal of Pediatrics, 147,* 335–340.

Meadan, H., Ostrosky, M. M., Zaghlawan, H. Y., & Yu, S. (2009). Promoting the social and communicative behavior of young children with autism spectrum disorders: A review of parent-implemented intervention studies. *Topics in Early Childhood Special Education, 29,* 90–104.

*Montgomery, P., Stores, G., & Wiggs, L. (2004). The relative efficacy of two brief treatments for sleep problems in young learning disabled (mentally retarded) children: A randomized controlled trial. *Archives of Disease in Childhood, 89,* 125–130.

Mullen, B. (1989). *Advanced BASIC meta-analysis.* Mahwah, NJ: Lawrence Erlbaum.

Oono, I. P., Honey, E. J., & McConachie, H. (2013) Parent-mediated early intervention for young children with autism spectrum disorders (ASD). *Cochrane Database of Systematic Reviews, 4,* Art. No.: CD009774. doi:10.1002/14651858. CD009774.pub2.

*Oosterling, I., Visser, J., Swinkels, S., Rommelse, N., Donders, R., Woudenberg, T., … Buitelaar, J. (2010). Randomized controlled trial of the focus parent training for toddlers with autism: 1-year outcome. *Journal of Autism and Developmental Disorders, 40,* 1447–1458.

Petrenko, C. (2013). A review of intervention programs to prevent and treat behavioral problems in young children with developmental disabilities. *Journal of Developmental and Physical Disabilities, 25,* 651–679.

*Pilarz, K. (2009). Evaluation of the efficacy of a seven week public school curriculum based DIR/Floortime parent training program for parents of children on the autism spectrum. Unpublished doctoral dissertation, Temple University, Philadelphia, PA.

*Plant, K. M., & Sanders, M. R. (2007). Reducing problem behavior during care-giving in families of preschool-aged children with developmental disabilities. *Research in Developmental Disabilities, 28,* 362–385.

Powell, D. R., (2013). Parenting intervention outcome studies: Research design considerations. *Parenting: Science & Practice, 13,* 266–284.

*Quinn, M., Carr, A., Carroll, L., & O'Sullivan, D. (2007). Parents Plus Programme I: Evaluation of its effectiveness for pre-school children with developmental disabilities and behavioural problems. *Journal of Applied Research in Intellectual Disabilities, 20*, 345–359.

Reichow, B. (2012). Overview of meta-analyses on Early Intensive Behavioral Intervention for young children with autism spectrum disorders. *Journal of Autism and Developmental Disorders, 42*, 512–520.

Roberts, M. Y, & Kaiser, A. P. (2011). The effectiveness of parent-implemented language interventions: A meta-analysis. *American Journal of Speech-Language Pathology, 20*, 180–199.

*Roberts, C., Mazzucchelli, T., Studman, L., & Sanders, M. R. (2006). Behavioral family intervention for children with developmental disabilities and behavioral problems. *Journal of Clinical Child and Adolescent Psychology, 35*, 180–193.

*Roberts, J., Williams, K., Carter, M., Evans, D., Parmenter, T., Silove, N., Clark, T., Warren, A. (2011). A randomised controlled trial of two early intervention programs for young children with autism: Centre-based with parent program and home based. *Research in Autism Spectrum Disorders, 5*, 1553–1566.

Rosenthal, R. (1979). The "file drawer problem" and tolerance for null results. *Psychological Bulletin, 86*, 638–641.

Rosenthal, R. (1991). *Meta-Analytic Procedures for Social Research* (1st ed.). Newbury Park, CA: Sage Publications, Inc.

Saito, A., Stickley, A., Haraguchi, H., Takahashi, H., Ishitobi, M., & Kamio, Y. (2017). Association between autistic traits in preschool children and later emotional/behavioral outcomes. *Journal of Autism and Developmental Disorders. 47*, 3333–3346.

Schultz, T., Schmidt, C., & Stichter, J. (2011). A review of parent education programs for parents of children with autism spectrum disorders. *Focus on Autism and Other Developmental Disabilities, 26*, 96–104.

Singer, G. H. S., Ethridge, B. L., & Aldana, S. I. (2007). Primary and secondary effects of parenting and stress management interventions for parents of children with developmental disabilities: A meta-analysis. *Mental Retardation and Developmental Disabilities Research Reviews, 13*, 357–369.

Smith, T. B., Oliver, M. N., & Innocenti, M. S. (2001). Parenting stress in families of children with disabilities. *American Journal of Orthopsychiatry, 71*(2), 257.

*Sofronoff, K., Attwood, T., Hinton, S., & Levin, I. (2007). A randomized controlled trial of a cognitive behavioural intervention for anger management in children diagnosed with Asperger syndrome. *Journal of Autism and Developmental Disorders, 37*, 1203–1214.

*Sofronoff, K., Leslie, A., Brown, W. (2004). Parent management training and Asperger syndrome. *Autism, 8*, 301–317.

*Solomon, M., Ono, M., Susna, T., & Goodlin-Jones, B. (2008). The effectiveness of parent-child interaction therapy for families of children on the autism spectrum. *Journal of Autism and Developmental Disorders, 38,* 1767–1776.

*Stahmer, A. C., & Gist, K. (2001). The effects of an accelerated parent education program on technique mastery and child outcome. *Journal of Positive Behavior Interventions, 3,* 75–82.

*Strauss, K., Vicari, S., Valeri, G., D'Elia, L., Arima, S., & Fava, L. (2012). Parent inclusion in early intensive behavioral intervention: The influence of parental stress, parent treatment fidelity and parent-mediated generalization of behavior targets on child outcomes. *Research in Developmental Disabilities, 33,* 688–703.

Sutton, A. J. (2009). Publication bias. In H. Cooper, L. V. Hedges, and J. Valentine (Eds.) *The handbook of research synthesis and meta-analysis* (pp. 435–452). New York, NY: Russell Sage Foundation.

Tellegen, C. L., & Sanders, M. R. (2013). Stepping Stones Triple P—Positive Parenting Program for children with disability: A systematic review and meta-analysis. *Research in Developmental Disabilities, 34,* 1556–1571.

Thomas, R., & Zimmer-Gembeck, M. J. (2007). Behavioral outcomes of Parent-Child Interaction Therapy and Triple P—Positive Parenting Program: A review and meta-analysis. *Journal of Abnormal Child Psychology, 35,* 475–495.

Tonge, B., Brereton, A., Kiomall, M., Mackinnon, A., King, N., & Rinehart, N. (2006). Effects on parental mental health of an education and skills training program for parents of young children with autism: A randomized controlled trial. *Journal of the American Academy of Child & Adolescent Psychiatry, 45,* 561–569.

Wade, C., Llewellyn, G., & Matthews, J. (2008). Review of parent training interventions for parents with intellectual disability. *Journal of Applied Research in Intellectual Disabilities, 21,* 351–366.

*Wade, S. L., Michaud, L., & Brown, T. M. (2006). Putting the pieces together: Preliminary efficacy of a family problem-solving intervention for children with traumatic brain injury. *Journal of Head Trauma Rehabilitation, 21,* 57–67.

Whittingham, K., Wee, D., & Boyd, R. (2011). Systematic review of the efficacy of parenting interventions for children with cerebral palsy. *Child: Care, Health and Development, 37,* 475–483.

*Wong, V. C., & Queenie, K. K. (2010). Randomized controlled trial for early intervention for autism: A pilot study of the autism 1-2-3 project. *Journal of Autism and Developmental Disorders, 40,* 677–688.

Woodman, A., & Hauser-Cram, P. (2013). The role of coping strategies in predicting change in parenting efficacy and depressive symptoms among mothers of adolescents with developmental disabilities. *Journal of Intellectual Disability Research, 57,* 513–530.

Xiong, N., Yang, L., Yu, Y., Hou, J., Li, J., Li, Y., … Jiao, Z. (2011). Investigation of raising burden of children with autism, physical disability and mental disability in China. *Research in Developmental Disabilities, 32,* 306–311.

*Yoder, P. J., & Warren, S. F. (2002). Effects of prelinguistic milieu teaching and parent responsivity education on dyads involving children with intellectual disabilities. *Journal of Speech, Language, and Hearing Research, 45,* 1158–1174.

# Contributors

**Vincent C. Alfonso**, Ph.D., is the dean of the School of Education at Gonzaga University. He is past president of Division 16 (School Psychology) of the American Psychological Association (APA), fellow of Divisions 5, 16, and 43 of the APA, and a certified school psychologist and licensed psychologist. Most recently, Dr. Alfonso received the Jack Bardon Distinguished Service Award from Division 16. He has been providing psychoeducational services to individuals across the life span for more than 25 years and is the coeditor of *Essentials of Specific Learning Disability Identification, 2nd edition*, and coauthor of *Essentials of Cross-Battery Assessment*, 3rd edition.

**Melody Boling** has worked in the field of social work for 31 years. During this time she has practiced in the field of Education, Healthcare, Mental Health, and Statewide systems capacity-building. She believes in the early childhood Arena that building holding environments that contain warm responsive interactions through a parallel process one can truly nurture and support a young child and their caregivers to thrive.

**Mark Matthew Buckman** is a doctoral student in the Department of Special Education at the University of Kansas. His work focuses on supporting schools in implementing comprehensive, integrated, three-tiered (Ci3T) models of prevention. His research interests include measurement of treatment integrity of schoolwide support models such as Ci3T, supporting in-service teachers in implementing evidence-based practices to support students' academic, social, and behavioral development, and behavior screening.

**Eric Alan Common** is an assistant professor at the University of Michigan-Flint. His work focuses on the active role schools play in child development and school-based prevention using tiered models to identify and support students at the earliest indication of need. More specifically, his research examines socio-emotional and behavior supports within comprehensive, integrated three-tiered models of prevention (Ci3T); and empowering educators to progress monitor intervention effectiveness by examining treatment integrity, social validity, and student outcome data in tandem.

Professor Common serves on the editorial boards of Behavioral Disorders and Journal of Positive Behavior Interventions, as well as a Special Issue Editor for Education and Treatment of Children.

**Cristy Coughlin**, Ph.D., received her doctorate in School Psychology from the University of Oregon and an undergraduate degree in Psychology from Western Michigan University. Coughlin has worked as a First Step coach, school-based behavioral consultant, and program evaluator for educational projects based in the United States, Australia, and Africa. Her areas of expertise include educational assessment, applied behavior analysis, and translating educational research to practice.

**Shantel Crosby** Ph.D., LCSW, is an assistant professor in the Kent School of Social Work at the University of Louisville. Dr. Crosby's on-going research interests include wellbeing and adverse childhood experiences among youth who are court-involved or at risk of court-involvement—particularly among youth of color. She focuses on trauma and behavioral/emotional health among this population and explores innovative and trauma-informed responses to maladaptive youth behaviors.

**Vicki Davolt** , LMSW, co-coordinates SOAR (System Offering Actions for Resilience in Early Childhood) located in Boone County, Missouri. She is the coordinator/behavioral consultant for the Early Childhood Positive Behavior Support (EC-PBS) program and a clinician with Child Parent Psychotherapy (CPP). She is committed to building community awareness and developing programs to promote the social-emotional wellness of children age 0-6 and their families.

**Tina Taylor Dyches** is a professor and associate dean in the McKay School of Education at Brigham Young University. Dr. Dyches' professional interests include family adaptation to children with disabilities and chronic conditions, and provision of appropriate services to individuals with disabilities and their families. She has published over 50 book chapters and refereed articles and has made over 180 professional presentations on topics related to students with disabilities. She is a co-founder of *Sibshops of Utah County* and collaborates with other organizations to provide this service to siblings of children with special needs.

**Wendy Ell**, OTR/L, is currently the E. Director of the Missouri Child Psychiatry Access Project (MO-CPAP) through the University of Missouri Department of Psychiatry. Wendy has over twenty year experience with children in various settings including early intervention, inpatient psychiatric care and in early childhood assessment and treatment. She advocates for coordination of care between all providers involved with individual children with the goal of assuring the best possible care and support for children.

**Edward G. Feil**, Ph.D., is an educational psychologist specializing in Early Intervention and Senior Research Scientist at the Oregon Research Institute. He is a coauthor of the First Step program and Early Screening Project and has extensive field experience with assessment and intervention with young children eligible for special education services. His research interests include (a) early childhood assessment methodology of psychopathology and intervention development for oppositional behavior disorders and (b) incorporating technology into the delivery of evidence-based interventions to hard-to-reach populations.

**Angel Fettig,** Ph.D., is an assistant professor of Special Education at the University of Washington. Her research focuses on supporting the social-emotional development and reducing challenging behaviors for young children with or at risk for disabilities. Specifically, Dr. Fettig examines factors that influence implementation and intervention fidelity for education professionals, parents, and caregivers in implementing evidence-based practices.

**Steve Forness** Ed.D., is Distinguished Professor Emeritus of Psychiatry and Biobehavioral Sciences at UCLA. He initially attended the U.S. Naval Academy, receiving his BA in 1963 and MA in 1964 from the University of Northern Colorado and his EdD in 1968 from UCLA. From 1968 to 2003, he was on the faculty of the UCLA Neuropsychiatric Hospital, where he was also principal of its hospital school and chief of educational psychology services. Dr. Forness has coauthored or coedited 10 books on children with learning or behavioral disorders and published more than 200 journal articles on special education and early detection of children with psychiatric disorders. He was a Fullbright Scholar in Portugal in 1976 and has received the Wallin Award from the Council for Exceptional Children and the Berman Award from the American Academy of Child and Adolescent Psychiatry.

**Andy Frey** is a professor at the University of Louisville, Kent School of Social Work. Dr. Frey's research focuses on school-based mental health and social work services, such as the First Step NEXT intervention, home-based approaches, and motivational interviewing within school settings.

**Annemieke Golly**, Ph.D., was born and raised in The Netherlands and is currently a research scientist at the Oregon Research Institute. As a certified special education teacher, she taught elementary students with special needs for 25 years. Dr. Golly received her Ph.D. in Special Education from the University of Oregon. Her areas of expertise are early and preventive intervention, behavior management, and classroom and schoolwide management. Dr. Golly has been instrumental in designing, implementing, and conducting nationwide research on the First Step program. She also has implemented behavior management strategies for pre-K through grade 12 across the United States, Canada, South Africa and Turkey. For the past 5 years, she has been training, coaching, and providing technical assistance to school and youth services staffs in the Netherlands for nationwide implementation of First Step and BEST Behavior, a K-12 positive behavior support program.

**Ambra L. Green**, Ph.D., is an assistant professor of Special Education and Special Education Program Director in the Department of Curriculum and Instruction within the College of Education at The University of Texas at Arlington. Her research focuses on diverse learners with and at-risk for disabilities, disproportionality within marginalized populations, the implementation of Positive Behavior Interventions and Supports, and educational policy as a means to mitigate systemic disparities. Prior to her work in higher education, Dr. Green was a special educator at the middle school level.

**Byran B. Korth** is an associate professor in Religious Education at Brigham Young University in Provo, Utah. From 1999-2004 he was the Director of Children's Programs of a large public-private early learning center managed by Auburn University. In 2004 he joined the faculty at BYU as the Early Childhood Education Program Coordinator. His teaching and scholarship has focused on preparing undergraduate students to be early childhood teachers in pre-K through 2nd grade early learning programs and public schools. He currently teaches undergraduate courses addressing the central purpose of families in our everyday lives.

**Rachel Kryah**, M.SW./M.PH., has over twelve years of experience in evaluation research. Ms. Kryah has been responsible for developing, managing, and leading large applied research projects that evaluate the effectiveness of national and state prevention and intervention grants for children, youth, and families, as well as providing program evaluation services to local school districts and agencies serving children and families. She has worked on several SAMHSA funded national longitudinal evaluations including the Starting Early Start Smart, Mentoring and Family Strengthening, Safe Schools/Healthy Students, Mental Health Transformation Statewide Incentive Grant, and Project LAUNCH, all funded by SAMHSA. Her work at the Missouri Institute of Mental Health (MIMH) at the University of Missouri–St. Louis has recently focused on evaluating Partnership for Success, a program addressing underage drinking and prescription drug misuse in youth across Missouri, funded by SAMHSA. She is also the evaluator for two local child wellness programs funded by the Boone County Children's Service Fund.

**Suzanne Kucharczyk**, Ed.D., is an assistant professor of Special Education at the University of Arkansas. Her research focuses on the expertise of families and professionals in their implementation of evidence based practices for children and youth with autism spectrum disorder and those with high support needs. Currently, Dr. Kucharczyk directs the *Teaming for Transition* program at the University of Arkansas in partnership with state and local transition leaders and stakeholders.

**Kathleen Lynne Lane** is a professor in the Department of Special Education at the University of Kansas. Dr. Lane's research interests focus on school-based interventions (academic and behavioral) with students at risk for emotional and behavioral disorders (EBD), with an emphasis on systematic screenings to detect students with behavioral challenges at the earliest possible juncture. She has designed, implemented, and evaluated comprehensive, integrated, three-tiered (CI3T) models of pre-vention in elementary, middle, and high school settings to (a) prevent the development of EBD and (b) responding to existing instances. Dr. Lane has served as the primary investigator for state and federally-funded projects including: Implementing Ci3T Models to Meet Students' Academic, Behavior, and Social Needs: A Researcher-Practitioner Partnership funded through the Institute of Educational Sciences (IES); Project Support and Include (PSI); Project WRITE, a Goal Area 2 Grant funded through the IES, focusing on impact of writing interventions for students at risk for EBD; an OSEP directed project studying positive behavior support at the high school level; and an OSEP field-initiated project studying prevention of EBD at the elementary level. She has expertise in school-based intervention and statistical analysis including multivariate analysis of longitudinal data sets. She is the co-editor of *Remedial and Special Education* and *Journal of Positive Behavior Intervention*. She also serves on several editorial boards including *Exceptional Children*, the *Journal of Special Education*, and *Journal of Emotional and Behavioral Disorders*. Dr. Lane has co-authored five books and published 133 refereed journal articles and 30 book chapters.

**Jon Lee** is currently an assistant professor of Early Childhood Education and Human Development at the University of Cincinnati, and a member of the Motivational Interviewing Network of Trainers (MINT). Jon continues to focus his research on the development social and behavioral interventions for young children in preschool and the primary grades, and the various applications of Motivational Interviewing in educational contexts.

**Barbara Mandleco** has been a nurse educator for over 45 years, has taught Families and Chronic Illness, Pediatric Nursing, Nursing Research, and Management of Families in the College of Nursing at Brigham Young

University. She is the recipient of numerous awards for her research and teaching and inducted into the Western Academy of Nursing. She has authored or co-authored 4 books, 33 book chapters, and 27 peer-reviewed publications. She also has made over 145 peer-reviewed presentations and has served several professional organizations in leadership positions.

**Jennifer M. McKenzie**, Ph.D., is an assistant professor of Special Education and Special Education Program Director in the Department of Teacher Education and Family Development within the College of Education and Human Development at Southern Utah University. Her research interests include evidence-based teacher preparation and coaching of inservice teachers, both as they relate to working with students with behavioral disorders. Prior to her work in higher education, Dr. McKenzie was a special educator, special education director, and special education compliance consultant.

**Wendy Peia Oakes** is an assistant professor at the Mary Lou Fulton Teachers College at Arizona State University. Her work focuses on practices that improve educational access and outcomes for young children with and at risk for emotional and behavioral disorders. For example, her research addresses school-wide systems based on comprehensive, integrated, three-tiered (Ci3T) models of prevention; the implementation of evidence-based academic and behavioral interventions; and professional development for preservice and in-service educators in implementing practices with fidelity. Professor Oakes serves as an associate editor for *Behavioral Disorders*, the *Journal of Positive Behavior Interventions*, and *Remedial and Special Education*, and *Special Issue Editor for Education and Treatment of Children*. She served as the President of the Council for Exceptional Children-Council for Children with Behavioral Disorders.

**Tia R. Schultz**, Ph.D., BCBA-D, is an associate professor of Special Education at the University of Wisconsin-Whitewater. Her professional work focuses on training and supporting parents and teachers to implement social and behavioral interventions for youth with and without identified disabilities. Currently, Dr. Schultz serves on the Treatment Intervention Advisory Committee (TIAC) for the state of WI.

**John Seeley**, Ph.D., is a professor in the Department of Special Education and Clinical Sciences at the University of Oregon and a senior research scientist at the Oregon Research Institute. His research interests include developmental psychopathology, prevention science, and school-based behavioral health intervention.

**Jason Small** is a senior data analyst at Oregon Research Institute. His research interests include behavioral screening and progress monitoring tools, tiered systems of support for students with emotional and behavioral difficulties, and research methodology. He has co-authored manuscripts on preventive behavioral interventions for young children, multiple-gating screening approaches, motivational interviewing, and psychopathology.

**Timothy B. Smith** is a professor in the Department of Counseling Psychology and Special Education, Brigham Young University, Provo, Utah.

**Marilyn Sprick**, M.S., is a consultant with Safe and Civil Schools and lead author of the *Read Well K–2 Reading Series*. Ms. Sprick is also author of "Intervention B: Academic Assistance" in *Interventions: Evidence-Based Behavioral Strategies for Individual Students* and a coauthor of *First Step Next, Meaningful Work, Tough Kid: On-Task in a Box*, and *SMART Kids: Social Grace, Manners, and Respectful Talk*. Marilyn is president of Pacific Northwest Publishing, a publishing house that focuses on highly effective, research-based resources for educators.

**Melissa A. Sreckovic**, Ph.D., is an assistant professor of Special Education at the University of Michigan-Flint. Her professional work focuses on examining the efficacy of social-behavioral interventions to support children and adolescents in inclusive settings. Currently, Dr. Sreckovic directs the Master of Arts in Inclusive Education program at the University of Michigan-Flint.

**Brianna Stiller**, Ph. D., was a School Psychologist for 32 years with School District 4J in Eugene, Or. She was co-author of three intervention programs, including First Step to Success, First Step Next, and Bully Prevention in Positive Behavior Support. She was awarded the Lifetime Achievement Award from the Northwest Positive Behavior Support Network in 2016, and the Lifetime Achievement Award for Eugene area educators from Oregon Community Credit Union in 2017.

**Melissa Stormont**, Ph.D., is a professor of Special Education at the University of Missouri-Columbia. Her research areas focus on the prevention of social emotional problems in young children and using systems approaches for supporting kindergarten readiness. Dr. Stormont has published extensive research on the educational and social needs of children at risk for failure in school. She has been a Co-PI on two efficacy trials to evaluate interventions and two personnel preparation grants to support graduate students in key need areas. She is also the mother of two children with ADHD and giftedness. Prior to her work in higher education, Dr. Stormont was a preschool teacher.

**Hill Walker** is Professor Emeritus in the College of Education at the University of Oregon. He is the founder and co-director of the U of O's Institute on Violence and Destructive behavior. His current research activities include early intervention for students with behavior disorders and strategies for making schools safer.

**Laine Young-Walker**, MD, is a Diplomate of the American Board of Psychiatry and Neurology in General Psychiatry as well as Child and Adolescent Psychiatry. She currently serves as Associate Dean for Student Programs at the School of Medicine, the Division Chief of Child and Adolescent Psychiatry, and is an Associate Professor of Psychiatry, at University of Missouri Health Care. She has worked locally to create programs which help children in the community. These include Bridge: School-Based Psychiatry, Early Childhood-Positive Behavior Supports program (EC-PBS), the System Offering Actions for Resilience (SOAR) in Early childhood and the Boone County: Early Child Coalition. Bridge provides early access in the schools for children in need of psychiatric assessment and treatment. EC-PBS/SOAR/ECC all focus on early childhood efforts including screening for social and emotional issues, working with childcare providers to increase their knowledge and skills in social and emotional development, providing an evidence based therapy for young children exposed to trauma and providing Triple P Interventions to young children and their families.

# GENERAL ARTICLE

# Kindergarten Readiness and Malleable Skill Deficits: Practical Considerations

*Melissa Stormont, Dan R. Cohen, and Aaron M. Thompson*

## Abstract

Many children enter kindergarten in need of support due to early social, emotional, and behavioral problems. The purpose of the current study is to contribute information on specific social competence skills (from the Teacher Observation of Child Adaptation-Revised [TOCA-R]) associated with poor readiness. Readiness was assessed using the Kindergarten Academic and Behavior Readiness Screener (K-ABRS), which consists of teacher-rated school readiness of a student when compared to his or her peers at that school. Participants in this study include 55 teachers and 893 kindergarten students from 18 elementary schools in one district located in a moderate-sized Midwestern city. Data were collected using the district's own online survey instrument. Students were assessed for six social-emotional skills; those who were rated poorly in readiness scored lower in these social competence skills than those rated average or above in readiness. Demographic characteristics were also related to social-emotional skills. Implications for connecting readiness with teachable skills are discussed.

Key words: readiness, social skills, prevention, challenging behavior

Estimates suggest 20% of students (e.g., two to three students per class) arrive at kindergarten with significant social, emotional, and behavioral problems (Centers for Disease Control and Prevention [CDC], 2013; Stormont, Herman, Reinke, King, & Owens, 2015), yet 80% of those students do not have access to effective supports (Essau, 2005; Kataoka, Zhang, & Wells, 2002). United States schools, as institutions, have a social responsibility and a legislatively-derived duty to promote the academic and social-emotional well-being of all students (Every Student Succeeds Act, 2016). To meet this responsibility and duty, educators have widely adopted tiered prevention models as an efficient means to identify, intervene, and monitor student behavioral health (Horner et al., 2009). Properly implemented and effective tiered prevention models (i.e., positive behavior and intervention supports [PBIS]) are predicated on the use of social, emotional, and behavioral data—including screening data—to identify at- and in-risk students, select a range of supports, and appraise the impact of those coordinated efforts over time (Horner et al., 2009).

A number of universal screening tools have been developed to identify children in need of further assessment and intervention in schools; however, the majority of this work has focused on academic risk and the development and testing of feasible social-emotional screening tools has lagged behind (Cook, Volpe, & Lavanis, 2010; Volpe et al., 2010). Given the opportunity and responsibility that schools have for identifying and supporting students with social-emotional needs, the purpose of the present study is to explore specific skills associated with overall readiness for kindergarten, which can be targeted for early intervention.

## Kindergarten Academic and Behavior Readiness Screener

The Kindergarten Academic and Behavior Readiness Screener (K-ABRS) allows a teacher to rate the school readiness of a student compared to his or her peers at that school. The screener has been tested in multiple studies in urban, suburban, and rural schools and has been documented to have strong psychometric properties (Stormont et al., 2015; Stormont, Thompson, Herman, & Reinke, 2017). Scores on the K-ABRS have also been shown to be predictive of reading performance on the Peer-Assisted Learning Strategies for Kindergarteners (K-PALs) (Stormont et al., 2017). Although readiness provides one useful metric for problem-solving teams and school personnel, for students in need of additional assessments and supports, it falls short in informing instructional needs.

Documentation of specific social competence skills associated with poor kindergarten readiness should be a key tool for any school-based problem-solving teams as they target supports for students using the K-ABRS. Specifically, for students rated in the "poor" range on the K-ABRS, a main purpose of this study is to explore and report skill deficits that are malleable. It is important to target those skills that are malleable, defined as those that can be influenced through instruction, in order to support the growth of resilience and readiness in students. Furthermore, a great deal of prior research has identified a host of moderating characteristics that influence school readiness, such as gender, poverty, and ethnicity/race (e.g., Stormont et al., 2015). Although for the most part these characteristics are not changeable, it is important to have this data to inform screening work. For example, it is well-documented that boys are often socially-emotionally and academically less ready for school compared to girls (Stormont et al., 2015). What does this mean in terms of specific skills that boys may need support to learn? Children raised in low-income homes are at increased risk for lack of readiness for kindergarten compared to their more affluent peers (Kataoka et al., 2002; Stormont et al., 2015). In addition, because of the well-documented overlap between being a member of a minority racial group and growing up in a low-income environment, this study also examines specific skill deficits associated with these characteristics. This information can be used to stress the need to target these skills to foster success for children.

## Method

### Participants

Participants in this study included 893 kindergarten students and 55 teachers in 18 elementary schools from one district located in a moderate-sized Midwestern city. Forty-eight percent of the student sample was female and 52% was male. English was a second language for 11% of the students, and school records indicated

44% participated in the subsidized lunch program. Students in the sample predominately identified as Caucasian (63%) or African American (21%) with modest representation of Asian (4%), Hispanic (5%), and Multiracial (6%) identities. Teacher participants were predominantly female (98%), and the majority held a master's degree (64.7%). Teachers reported an average of 10.2 years ($SD$ = 4.78) of experience with an average age being 36 years ($SD$ =5.6). Almost all of the teachers (98%), identified as European American or Caucasian.

## Procedures

The school district and the university where this work originated approved all study procedures. Administrators contacted all kindergarten teachers in the district ($n$ =71) and asked them to participate in the study; after the invitation to participate, 78% of teachers ($n$ = 55) provided consent and participated; 22% declined. Teacher participants completed the measures described below for all students. Data were collected using the district's own online survey instrument and teachers received $40 for completing the survey. District data managers merged all student data.

## Measures

**Social-emotional readiness.** Social-emotional readiness was assessed using a previously validated and reduced version of the Teacher Observation of Child Adaptation-Revised (TOCA-R; Werthamer-Larsson, Kellam, & Wheeler, 1991). Specifically, we relied on items from the authority acceptance, social competence, and emotional regulation subscales of the TOCA-R. The items are rated from 1 (never) to 7 (always) and negatively worded items were reverse coded so higher scores reflected increased school readiness (e.g., fights = 1 recoded to = 7) before composite scale scores were computed. Similar to prior studies (e.g., Thompson, 2014), the scales demonstrated excellent internal consistency in the present sample data ($a$ = .92 –.96). In terms of predictive validity, in a sample of 2,145 third through fifth grade students, screening scores of the most at-risk students (i.e., 20% of students) predicted poor scores on math ($F[2,143]=202.095, p<.001$) and reading achievement tests ($F[2,143]=184.014, p<.001$; Thompson, 2014).

**Overall school readiness item from the K-ABRS**. The K-ABRS overall readiness item is a single item and teachers respond to the following prompt, "*Please rate this child's overall school readiness compared to his or her peers*" using a ten-point scale (0 = *not ready*, 10 = *ready*). Prior studies of the reliability and predictive validity of the K-ABRS have tested various response formats (e.g., 5-point scale, Stormont et al., 2015; 10-point scale; Stormont et al., 2017) and the item—regardless of the response format—demonstrates strong concurrent and predictive validity for student academic and behavior outcomes (Stormont et al., 2015).

## Data Analysis

As expected, the distribution of the social-emotional readiness TOCA-R items did not meet assumptions of equality of variance, thus violating major assumptions associated with analysis of variance (ANOVA), a common method for assessing group differences. Therefore, the non-parametric Kruskal-Wallis test, which does not include assumptions of normality and homogeneity of variance, was used to evaluate median differences across groups. Analyses were carried out with several categorical demographic variables and a binary indicator of school readiness using Statistical Package for the Social Sciences (SPSS) version 23. In order to model the interaction between race and free and reduced-rate lunch (FRL) using the c Kruskal-Wallis test, a four-category variable was constructed to represent the association between item scores and the four possible combinations of race and FRL status. These analyses yield three important pieces of information: the median item score based on group assignment; the mean rank, which is generated by ranking the item scores and computing the mean based on group assignment; and an H test which evaluates whether the differences between mean rank scores across groups is statistically significant.

To correct for type 1 error given the number of tests conducted, the significance value of .01 was selected for all statistical tests (McCoach et al., 2010).

# Results

There was a statistically significant difference between students classified by their teacher as ready or not ready for all skills including: follows directions ($H(1, 2) = 174.98, p < .001$), works well alone ($H(1, 2) = 246.04, p < .001$), persists at challenging tasks ($H(1, 2) = 234.29, p < .001$), works well with others ($H(1, 2) = 147.88, p < .001$), solves problems on their own ($H(1, 2) = 184.01, p < .001$) and helps others ($H(1, 2) = 130.34, p < .001$). Table 1 provides median item values based on readiness and associated mean rank scores.

There was also a statistically significant difference between female and male students for all of the social-emotional and regulation skills assessed. That is, males had significantly poorer scores than female students on the TOCA-R items follows directions ($H(1, 2) = 27.04, p <.001$), works well alone ($H(1, 2 ) = 25.30, p <.001$), persists at challenging tasks ($H(1, 2) = 31.58, p < .001$), works well with others ($H(1, 2) = 29.59, p <.001$), solves problems on their own ($H(1, 2) = 25.28, p <.001$) and helps others ($H(1, 2) = 33.31, p <.001$). Table 2 provides median item values based on sex and associated mean rank scores.

Multiple categories were generated to model the interaction between race and FRL. There was a statistically significant difference between Caucasian students without FRL and African American students with FRL for all skills assessed including: follows directions ($H(1, 2) = 45.14, p <.001$), works well alone ($H(1, 2) = 43.08, p <.001$), persists at challenging tasks ($H(1, 2) = 47.76, p <.001$), works well with others ($H(1, 2) = 23.36, p <.001$), solves problems on their own ($H(1, 2) = 21.32, p <.001$) and helps others ($H(1, 2) = 9.97, p =.002$). No statistically significant differences were found between African American students with and without FRL and between Caucasian and African American students with FRL. Table 3 provides median item values based on the race/FRL interaction and associated mean rank scores.

# Discussion

This study documented specific social skills associated with a single item of overall kindergarten readiness. Demographic data were also analyzed and results showed that gender and FRL eligibility were important to measure as associated characteristics of children who are more likely to enter school with readiness deficits. Furthermore, there were differences between Caucasian students who did not receive FRL and African American students who did receive FRL; future research needs to replicate and extend this research using measures beyond teacher ratings.

## Implications

Researchers in this study sought to go beyond conceptualizing kindergarten readiness from a descriptive lens and target what amendable skills are associated with readiness deficits. If students were rated as not ready for kindergarten, then they also had significantly lower social-emotional skills on the TOCA-R including following directions, working well alone, persisting at challenging tasks, working well with others, solving problems on their own, and helping others. Female students were rated higher on these social-emotional skills than male students. When race (African American, Caucasian) and FRL (yes or no) were considered together, Caucasian students who did not qualify for FRL had higher scores than African American students who did qualify for FRL on all six skills assessed. No other differences were documented.

In terms of teachable skills to support, this study found specific social skills were less developed in students who were not ready for kindergarten. When considering supports for teachable skills, it is prudent to consider how these proposed supports align with a multi-tiered system of existing supports. For example, for universal supports in kindergarten, all students need to receive specific instruction on social skills to be successful. All of the assessed skills from this research could be easily included in a matrix of school expectations. Students who are rated by their teacher as being "not ready" on the K-ABRS may also need secondary supports to increase their likelihood of successful acquisition and use of skills. These supports could include pre-corrective statements, behavior-specific praise, and visuals to remind students of specific steps. For example, if solving problems is the skill then a framework for problem solving could be included on a poster and/or visual taped to the student's desk.

Demographic characteristics were also associated with each of the social, emotional, and regulation skills assessed. Indeed, it is important to note that prior studies have noted implicit bias concerns, when relying on teacher nomination, in the ratings of behaviors in students of varying backgrounds and skin color. For example, the cumulative effect of being a male and African American has been shown to increase the risk of teacher bias on measures of student behavior (Downer, Goble, Myers, & Pianta, 2016; Gilliam, Maupin, Reyes, Accavitti, & Shic, 2016). African American students who did not have FRL status did not differ from Caucasian students with or without FRL or from their African American peers in terms of their scores on social-emotional readiness items. These data can inform school personnel who work with high proportions of students who are African American and receive FRL to increase efforts to screen and intervene in social skills early in kindergarten. Data also inform educators and researchers that poverty continues to be an important risk factor to consider in supporting students; thus, offering additional support to existing efforts to provide assessment and intervention resources to high poverty populations seems necessary.

Gender differences documented in this study also inform readiness research. Specifically, males are more likely to have lower ratings than females related to specific social skills. Thus, rather than simply describing males as less mature, it is important to think of readiness as something related to teachable skills.

## Limitations of the Study

There are important limitations for this study. First, the participants were from one school district in a Midwestern state and the results may not generalize to other regions. Second, teacher reports were used as the main variables for the study; future research should utilize other measures, including direct observation. Third, readiness should be measured in a social-ecological framework to ascertain who is at risk and under what circumstances. Fourth, one screening item, rated by one person, should not be used to make decisions regarding referral or classification purposes. Multiple sources of data should always be used when making important decisions about students' risk. And, lastly, the analyses presented here do not control for the nesting structure of students in classrooms, or of classrooms in schools, and the use of multiple tests to examine differences by group may inflate the type 1 error rate. To adjust for concerns related to this factor, we elected to rely on a .01 probability value—however, there is still a 1 % chance that the associations reported here occurred by chance alone and are not due to real observed differences.

## Conclusions

Kindergarten entry is an important time for universal screening and interventions for young students who lack specific skills associated with success in school. It is imperative that research inform education professionals of teachable skills related to readiness that can be targeted for intervention. This study helps direct these efforts by highlighting six skills students who are low in readiness manifest in schools, according to their teachers.

### References

Centers for Disease Control and Prevention (2013). Mental health surveillance among children—United States, 2005–2011. *Morbidity and Mortality Weekly Report,* *62,* 1–35. Retrieved from www.cdc.gov

Cook, C., Volpe, R. J., & Lavanis, A. (2010). Constructing a roadmap for future universal screening research beyond academics. *Assessment for Effective Intervention, 35*, 198–206.

Downer, J. T., Goble, P., Myers, S. S., & Pianta, R. C. (2016). Teacher-child racial/ethnic match within pre-kindergarten classrooms and children's early school adjustment. *Early Childhood Research Quarterly, 37*, 26–38.

Essau, C. A. (2005). Frequency and patterns of mental health services utilization among adolescents with anxiety and depressive disorders. *Depression and Anxiety, 22*(3), 130–137.

Every Student Succeeds Act, S. 1177, 114th Congress, 2nd Sess. (2016).

Gilliam, W. S., Maupin, A. N., Reyes, C. R., Accavitti, M., & Shic, F. (2016). Do early educators' implicit biases regarding sex and race relate to behavior expectations and recommendations of preschool expulsions and suspensions? *Yale Child Study Center*, 9901–1013.

Horner, R. H., Sugai, G., Smolkowski, K., Eber, L., Nakasato, J., Todd, A. W., & Esperanza, J. (2009). A randomized, wait-list controlled effectiveness trial assessing school-wide positive behavior support in elementary schools. *Journal of Positive Behavior, 11*, 133–144.

Kataoka, S. H., Zhang, L., & Wells, K. B. (2002). Unmet need for mental health care among US children: Variation by ethnicity and insurance status. *American Journal of Psychiatry, 159*(9), 1548–1555.

McCoach, D. B., Goldstein, J., Behuniak, P., Reis, S. M., Black, A. C., Sullivan, E. E., & Rambo, K. (2010). Examining the unexpected: Outlier analyses of factors affecting student achievement. *Journal of Advanced Academics, 21*(3), 426–468.

Stormont, M., Herman, K. E., Reinke, W. M., King, K., & Owens, S. (2015). The kindergarten academic and behavior readiness screener: The utility of single item teacher ratings of kindergarten readiness. *School Psychology Quarterly, 30*, 212–228.

Stormont, M., Thompson, A., Herman, K., & Reinke, W. M. (2017). The social and emotional dimensions of a single item overall school readiness screener and its relations with academic outcomes. *Assessment for Effective Intervention, 42*, 67–76.

Thompson, A. M. (2014). Randomized trial of the Self-management Training And Regulation Strategy (STARS) for disruptive students. *Research on Social Work Practice, 24*, 414–427.

Volpe, R. J., Briesch, A. M., & Chafouleas, S. M. (2010). Linking screening for emotional and behavioral problems to problem-solving efforts: An adaptive model of behavioral assessment. *Assessment for Effective Intervention, 35*, 240–244.

Werthamer-Larsson, L., Kellam, S., & Wheeler, L. (1991). Effect of first-grade classroom environment on shy behavior, aggressive behavior, and concentration problems. *American Journal of Community Psychology, 19*(4), 585–602.

### Table 1.
### TOCA-R Item Score Medians and Kruskal–Wallis Mean Ranks by Readiness Status

|  | Ready (N=756) | | Not ready (N=137) | |
| --- | --- | --- | --- | --- |
|  | Median | Mean Rank | Median | Mean rank |
| Follows directions | 6.0 | 494.01 | 4.0 | 187.56 |
| Works well alone | 6.0 | 502.82 | 3.0 | 138.98 |
| Persists at challenging tasks | 6.0 | 502.20 | 3.0 | 142.42 |
| Works well with others | 6.0 | 490.24 | 4.0 | 208.39 |
| Solves problems on their own | 5.0 | 495.94 | 3.0 | 176.96 |
| Helps others | 6.0 | 488.02 | 4.0 | 220.65 |

*Note. TOCA-R Item scores range from 1-6 with higher scores indicating higher levels of social–emotional readiness. Medians and mean ranks reflect the midpoint value and average case rank in each category.*

### Table 2.
### TOCA-R Item Score Medians and Kruskal–Wallis Mean Ranks by Sex

|  | Female (N=430) | | Male (N=1463) | |
| --- | --- | --- | --- | --- |
|  | Median | Mean Rank | Median | Mean rank |
| Follows directions | 6.0 | 492.05 | 6.0 | 405.16 |
| Works well alone | 6.0 | 490.63 | 6.0 | 406.48 |
| Persists at challenging tasks | 6.0 | 496.40 | 5.0 | 401.12 |
| Works well with others | 6.0 | 494.15 | 6.0 | 403.21 |
| Solves problems on their own | 5.0 | 491.22 | 4.0 | 405.94 |
| Helps others | 6.0 | 497.55 | 5.0 | 400.06 |

*Note. TOCA-R Item scores range from 1-6 with higher scores indicating higher levels of social–emotional readiness. Medians and mean ranks reflect the midpoint value and average case rank in each category.*

**Table 3.**
*TOCA-R Item Score Medians and Kruskal–Wallis Mean Ranks by Race/FRL*

|  | Caucasian/no FRL (N=414) | | Caucasian/FRL (N = 146) | |
|---|---|---|---|---|
|  | Median | Mean Rank | Median | Mean Rank |
| Follows directions | 6.0 | 427.14 | 5.0 | 315.13 |
| Works well alone | 6.0 | 422.88 | 6.0 | 328.25 |
| Persists at challenging tasks | 6.0 | 425.29 | 5.0 | 322.52 |
| Works well with others | 6.0 | 409.08 | 6.0 | 332.04 |
| Solves problems on their own | 6.0 | 403.11 | 4.0 | 355.08 |
| Helps others | 6.0 | 395.60 | 5.0 | 357.74 |
|  | African American/no FRL (N=24) | | African American/FRL (N = 162) | |
|  | Median | Mean Rank | Median | Mean Rank |
| Follows directions | 5.5 | 310.65 | 5.0 | 298.33 |
| Works well alone | 5.5 | 309.65 | 5.0 | 297.54 |
| Persists at challenging tasks | 5.0 | 344.54 | 4.0 | 291.40 |
| Works well with others | 6.0 | 396.65 | 5.5 | 316.50 |
| Solves problems on their own | 4.0 | 378.15 | 4.0 | 313.74 |
| Helps others | 5.0 | 358.54 | 5.0 | 333.43 |

*Note. TOCA-R Item scores range from 1-6 with higher scores indicating higher levels of social–emotional readiness. Medians and mean ranks reflect the midpoint value and average case rank in each category.*

# Contributors

**Dan R. Cohen**, Ph.D., is a postdoctoral fellow at the Missouri Prevention Center at the University of Missouri-Columbia. He completed a master of public health at Johns Hopkins Bloomberg Public Health and a doctorate in school psychology at the University of Missouri-Columbia. His interests include school mental health, behavioral assessment, and disparities in school discipline and achievement.

**Melissa Stormont**, Ph.D., is a professor of Special Education at the University of Missouri-Columbia. Her research areas focus on the prevention of social emotional problems in young children and using systems approaches for supporting kindergarten readiness. Dr. Stormont has published extensive research on the educational and social needs of children at risk for failure in school. She has been a Co-PI on two efficacy trials to evaluate interventions and two personnel preparation grants to support graduate students in key need areas. She is also the mother of two children with ADHD and giftedness. Prior to her work in higher education, Dr. Stormont was a preschool teacher.

**Aaron M. Thompson**, Ph.D., M.SW., completed his doctorate in Social Work at the University of North Carolina, Chapel Hill. Prior to this, Aaron worked as a counselor and classroom teacher in a juvenile detention facility, an educational disability evaluation specialist in a clinical setting, and as a social worker and principal in a public school setting. Presently, Aaron is an Associate Professor in the School of Social Work at the University of Missouri and the Associate Director of the Missouri Prevention Center. Aaron's research and practice interests include the etiology of social, emotional, and behavioral health problems among school-aged youth; pre- and in-service training for social workers working in school settings; and the development and evaluation of effective prevention and intervention efforts to improve school readiness, self-regulation, and functioning of high risk youth and families through school based and school-community linked service models.

# Perspectives on
# Early Childhood Psychology and Education

*PECPE* publishes twice a year, in the fall and spring. These two special issues on specific topics are edited by one of the journal's associate editors, and also include a few general articles.

## Editorial Policy and Submission Guidelines

*Perspectives on Early Childhood Psychology and Education* focuses on publishing original contributions from a broad range of psychological and educational perspectives relevant to infants, young children (to age 8 years), families, and caregivers. Manuscripts incorporating evidence-based research, theory, and practice within clinical, community, developmental, neurological, and school psychology perspectives are considered. In addition, the journal accepts test and book reviews, literature reviews, program descriptions and evaluations, clinical studies, and other professional materials of interest to psychologists and educators working with young children. Proposals for special focus topics may be made to the Editor.

**Format:** Manuscripts should be original work not currently submitted for publication to other journals. Authors must follow the guidelines of the *Publication Manual of the American Psychological Association* (Sixth Edition). Manuscripts may not exceed 35 double-spaced pages in length, including the cover page, abstract, references, tables, and figures.

**Submission:** Submit an electronic copy of the manuscript for editorial review. Avoid including any identifying author information in the text. Selection of manuscripts is based on blind peer review. Include a cover page with the following information: the title of article, author(s) full name(s), title(s), institution or professional affiliations, and mailing and email address of primary author. The cover page will not be sent to reviewers.

## Selection Criteria:

- Importance of topic in early childhood psychology and education
- Theory and research related to content
- Contribution to professional practice in early childhood psychology and education
- Clear and concise writing

Submit manuscripts to the Editor at the following address:

Dr. Vincent C. Alfonso
Gonzaga University
School of Education
502 East Boone Avenue
Spokane, WA 99258

Email: PECPE@gonzaga.edu

# CALL FOR PAPERS

We are seeking a special focus for the Fall 2018 issue of *PECPE*. If you are interested in submitting a topic and being the guest editor, please send a brief (approximately 250 words) proposal to me, Dr. Vincent C. Alfonso, Editor, *PECPE*: PECPE@gonzaga.edu or alfonso@gonzaga.edu, for consideration.

Special focus and general manuscripts for the Fall 2018 issue are due **August 15, 2018**. Manuscripts should be original work not currently submitted for publication to other journals. Authors must follow the guidelines of the *Publication Manual of the American Psychological Association* (Sixth Edition). Manuscripts may not exceed 35 double-spaced pages in length, including the cover page, abstract, references, tables, and figures. Avoid including any identifying author information in the text. Selection of manuscripts is based on blind peer review. Include a cover page with the following information: the title of article, author(s) full name(s), title(s), institution or professional affiliations, and mailing and email address of primary author. The cover page will not be sent to reviewers.

Please share this information with your colleagues and students.

Volume 3, Issue 1 of
*Perspectives on Early Childhood Psychology and Education*
was published in Spring 2018
by Pace University Press


Cover and Interior Design by Sara Yager
Cover and Interior Layout by Bryan Potts
The journal was typeset in Minion and Myriad
and printed by Lightning Source in La Vergne, Tennessee

## Pace University Press

Director: Sherman Raskin
Associate Director: Manuela Soares
Marketing Manager: Patricia Hinds
Design Consultant: Sara Yager

Graduate Assistants: Bryan Potts and Elliane Mellet
Student Aide: Erica Magrin

www.ingramcontent.com/pod-product-compliance
Lightning Source LLC
Chambersburg PA
CBHW071121280326
41935CB00010B/1083